LIBERTY FROM DRUG ADDICTION
Live life with a different set of Rules

Power for the tormented souls

"An exposé on substance abuse and the irrevocable laws governing humanity"

-Know what you are dealing with to be free again-

Sydney M. Modise

First Edition 2023

ISBN: 978-0-6397-5330-0 (Paperback)

ISBN: 978-0-6397-5331-7 (eBook)

For more information visit: www.libertythebook.com

Contact: info@libertythebook.com

DISCLAIMER AND/OR LEGAL NOTICES:

The information presented herein represents the view of the author as of the date of publication. Because of the rate with which conditions change, the author reserves the right to alter and update his opinion based on the new conditions.

The lesson guide is for informational purposes only. While every attempt has been made to verify the information provided in this report, neither the author nor his affiliates/partners assume any responsibility for errors, inaccuracies, or omissions. Any slights of people or organizations are unintentional. If advice concerning legal or related matters is needed, the services of a fully qualified professional should be sought. This guide is not intended for use as a source of legal or accounting advice. You should be aware of any laws which govern business transactions or other business practices in your country and state. Any reference to any person or business whether living or dead is purely unintentional.

Dedication

"Give thanks to the LORD and proclaim his greatness. Let the whole world know what he has done." – Psalms 105:1 NLT
"Giving thanks is a sacrifice that truly honors Me. If you keep to My path, I will reveal to you the salvation of God." – Psalms 50:23 NLT

This book is dedicated to the Word of my heavenly Father, My Creator, The Strength of my Life. I thank The Lord for insight, knowledge, wisdom, and guidance in writing and accomplishing this material, as it is His will for my life to be a blessing to His beloved children. God has blessed me beyond measure. He has pulled me out of all sorts of unfavorable circumstances, even if it was by my own doing, and has made me rest in His marvelous Light. I exalt the Name of my Lord and Savior, Jesus Christ.

I thank my wife and kids for their unconditional love. They are a blessing and a gift in my life. I can never give enough thanks to my spiritual leader in the Lord, my Pastor, Lawrence Achiboye CA. I thank the ministry for the continued love, support, and training in the Lord.

The material in this book is not the opinion of, nor underwritten by any member or leader of the church. Therefore, the ministry is and should not be held liable for any information herein, or persecuted, nor be linked to any negative publication or hype generated from this writing. It is all my experience and opinion, and therefore all aspects of this script and anything circumstantial, especially negative, that arise from herein is accountable to me the author. I am a member of the church, and how I interpret the teachings is not anybody's liability but mine. However, if the teaching works out and is good for me, then it will certainly be profitable to you also, and thus the church should be credited as a good place to learn the word of God.

To my late dearest grandmother, I am grateful to you for showing me the way of love. You were impartial in raising all your children. Strong-willed you were. You fed and encouraged me to succeed no matter what comes my way. You are always in my heart.

I praise God that this book has reached you, the intended recipient. It will impact you in a most profound way that will help and bless your life. You will have a divine experience as you read, study, and understand the content. You are blessed.

Contents

Preface

Drug addiction is a complex and devastating problem that affects millions of individuals and families around the world. It can be a chronic and often relapsing condition that not only impacts physical and mental health, but can also have social, economic, and legal consequences. Despite its prevalence and significant impact, addiction is often misunderstood and stigmatized, and the essence of this dilemma is largely inadequately addressed to those addicted to drugs. The scientific and anatomical approach to explaining how drugs affect the human body only sparks the intellectual prowess of an individual if at all, however, there are several things at play in the background that needs to be addressed for a complete recovery inspired from within. You cannot force someone to quit drugs, and even those who wish to quit can sometimes find it an impossible mission, they then give in. This affects people from all walks of life, you'd be surprised; from presidents to beggars on the street, hence it's a multibillion-dollar business. The product flies off the shelves, better than sugar.

The key to absolute freedom is to be empowered with "Revelation Knowledge and Wisdom" in what you are dealing with. The medical institutions, rehabilitation centres, and professionals in this regard can only try to help you. God calls them His army. Yet, you can't resolve spiritual matters with physical or natural solutions. Consequently, we generally see numerous cases of relapses, and this is evident that the individuals' comprehension of addiction is not met. It is that which you do not know or are conscious of, and it cannot help you but can be unfavorable to your success and well-being. This translates to awareness and empowerment of one's emotional (soul) intelligence, physical intelligence, and most importantly spiritual intelligence.

The theme here doesn't disregard science, nor translate it as insignificant, I love the subject, but we go beyond the headlines. The universe and all that is in it is governed by forces set in place as laws, some of these laws supersede others, and the reality is you cannot change them: you either work with them or against them, and subsequently to your peril or success. Science is the study of things already in existence, creating and testing theories to pursue signs and wonders with the intent to harness the energy of that subject matter discovered, then to develop and benefit the human progression. Is this not faith in action?

Faith gets you excited when you are on to something, you become relentless on your pursuit because you believe so much in what you are trying to accomplish. Scientists are faithful servants acting out their belief in what God had already pointed out.

"Call unto me, and I will answer thee, and shew thee great and mighty things, which thou knowest not." – Jeremiah 33:3

This book is inspired by years of self-introspective episodes and journaling during an addiction struggle with cocaine and ketamine, which I later compiled and developed to share and help disseminate this bug to those who seem to be struggling. Having an analytical disposition and willpower to survive is what brought about the note-taking and questions because the severity of the situation was overbearing: You end up living for the next line. Nothing made sense, and neither could I help myself, but God revealed a bigger picture than I could fathom.

"Behold, I will bring it health and cure, and I will cure them, and will reveal unto them the abundance of peace and truth. And I will cleanse them from all their iniquity, whereby they have sinned against me; and I will pardon all their iniquities, whereby they have sinned, and whereby they have transgressed against me. And it shall be to me a name of joy, a praise and an honour before all the nations of the earth." – Jeremiah 33:6,8,9

This is my testimony presented in a "How-to-Manual". If you are tired of substance abuse, and you are thirsty for restoration, yearning to be free again, this is for you!

CHAPTER 1

Relationship with Substance

H ave you ever been in a relationship that seemed perfect at first, but as time went on, it took over your life and consumed you? That's exactly what happens when you hit it off with drugs. The initial thrill and pleasure turn into a dangerous and destructive dependence. As in any relationship, there is an initial point of contact between parties. Exciting new relationships tend to disrupt the general routine of one's life. A boy meets a girl, they fall in love, and sooner or later their friends start missing them because love has taken over the usual activities. The couple will invest a lot in the relationship, even their hard-earned money. This includes dealing with emotional issues, compromising character traits at times, and career paths, then future prospects are altered from promises made with the hope of things working out for the best – all in good faith. This goes on till vows are made, for better or for worse, and the two become one.

It's quite tricky to abandon an addictive habit, especially when it has a hold on you and invigorates your spirit, whether it's good for you or not. From your first contact with drugs, you may develop a strong relationship of dependency on the substance. From sunset to sunrise, you just must have a bag of coke or whatever illicit drug you are taking. It becomes evident that you feel you can't do without another line of cocaine. Thus, there can be a lot of alienation from what you used to do and who you used to be. Years go by, you lose time, ability, and potential.

When you pay proper attention, you find there is a particular bond or an embarrassing loyalty you have to the substance. How loyal can you be to something that causes harm to your physical appearance, overall health, and self-esteem?

For example, consider a group of close friends who have been using drugs together since they were young. When the availability of drugs is limited, they may turn against each other, using manipulation and abandonment to get their hands on the substance. You see lots of back-chatting among a group of addicts, and this is always in favor of obtaining a line or two. At this point, one would protect and secure a line of cocaine at all costs. A solid relationship has been established.

Although things may have appeared positive, the reality of the situation is not as rosy as it may have seemed in the beginning. The thrill and excursions may fade over time. The bond with drugs is often tumultuous and can involve both love and hate. Unfortunately, it can also be self-destructive and potentially fatal.

The first few times you hit was like you were invincible. You had an above-average sense of confidence, a manner of love towards everyone, chatting yourself away in a particularly higher consciousness. Possibilities were endless, like a person in love. The ecstatic feeling was out of this world. Sensual urges profoundly centered your being. A good conversation with line after line made the night seem short. But dawn after dawn, you started hating the birds chirping and the sun rising. This makes you realize that your inner core has been rearranged.

With every new day, people appreciate an endless dawning of possibilities, but you, on the other hand, detest having to face the day and all those sober, bright people – let alone yourself in the mirror. It gets even worse when the drugs demand more of you. That's the type of relationship you got yourself into, with a partner who doesn't give but only takes. It's a one-way traffic, down way under to an abyss.

Generally, relationships are a give-and-take. A con artist would knock on your door, obliviously you let him in, and he becomes your best acquaintance if not a friend but then comes the day when you lose everything and you regret that moment you opened the door for that person. What you deal with when you take drugs isn't merely a white powder that helps you cope with the waves of life. It's much more than meets the eye – or rather nose. It is something you can't see, but it has so much impact on you and about you. In this history of consuming drugs, you are certain there is an element of the supernatural. The question is, what have you allowed to come into your life? Surely a line of white powder just can't change so much about you!

What are drugs?
- These are termed social and mind-altering substances used and perceived for pleasure; Cocaine, Blow, Lala, Rock, Heroin, Acid, LSD, Ecstasy, Mali, Kat, Crystal Math, Tik, you can name them, the list is endless.
- But the ancient Greek translates pharmacy; the use of drugs or medicine, to pharmakeia: sorcery

What happens when you take drugs? You get high, and then later you come down from the high, then your life changes for the worst.

Here's a quick overview of the High and Low state of mind when riding this wave:

High State - Your thought process and heart rate are at their all-time high and sharp. You might feel lightheadedness or a head rush depending on what you take; an upper like cocaine or ketamine (the main ingredient being ephedrine), or a downer like crack cocaine or heroin. You are either too calm or too hyperactive but feel energized at the same time. You feel a sense of heightened confidence, brain power, and apparent moments of clarity, feeling relaxed and experiencing ecstatic bliss, and erotic desires are intense. You get very talkative, wide awake, you don't sleep, you don't eat, and hardly get hungry. You feel daring, and a good boost to your willpower. But these slightly differ from person to person.

Low State or downer(side-effects) - The higher you get, the harder the downer when the substance eases off from your system. You become tense and feel head, shoulder, and chest heavy. Your body becomes stiff. You feel drained in your body, soul, and spirit. The thought process gets slower and extremely focused but stagnant, from a negatively perceived disposition. Then hallucination kicks in, you start making things up in your head, and you become anxious and paranoid. You can't sleep even if you wanted. You become fearful and your willpower dissipates. This becomes an unhappy reality till you fall asleep.

Now let's examine how the above effects affect you (getting high all the time and getting low every morning). These characteristics you acquaint yourself with and practice, become a habit. You will experience them more and more till they become a norm – an encouraged second nature. Unfortunately, you are not designed to function like this; to artificially boost and modify your biological architecture with foreign substances on a daily.

This causes dysfunction, and here it is.

- A prolonged and elevated heart rate can lead to heart disease and potentially heart failure. Tachycardia is when your heart beats faster than normal, usually above 100 beats per minute. Now when the workload on your heart becomes overbearing, it can cause the heart muscle to become weak – Overdosing on the drug is the number one killer.

- Your thought process should not be at rapid levels, except for the occasional handling of tasks, of which you get breaks thereafter. With substance abuse on the other hand, leads to a lack of focus due to darting thoughts and rumination within short periods because the drugs affect the central nervous system including the parts of the brain responsible for speech and language, and if prolonged, it might lead to speech discord – incoherent and slurry speech.

- You can neither be healthy without a proper diet – drugs cause an abnormal loss of appetite for food leading to anorexia, gums, and skin disease.
- Prolonged brain hyperactivity with lack of sleep causes chemical imbalance, instability, and paranoia.
- A perverted mind is quite undesirable to many, one should not be thinking about sex all the time, as it causes challenges mentally, bodily, and in relationships.
- Being anxious and fearful affects willpower. Your willpower gives you the courage to do things that makes you grow, and growth is a prerequisite to life fulfillment.

The high state of mind that is induced by drugs is unsustainable, that is why it's always followed by crashing. When you are coming down (and this is not being calm, but rather a trip), your state of mind tries to mimic your normal sobriety state because your whole self-being is trying to pull you towards reality and needs a break at the same time. Later we will discuss what your self-being needs a break from.

In other words, the state of mind that will prevail (between high and low) is the one your body can closely relate to, even if it's not your true state of self. The pleasures you get from being high are abnormal, and they continually decrease, likewise as your dopamine levels are shut down. Then the morbid low state bounces back and forth with time when you are getting sober and settles on the previous high-low. Your personality becomes your lowest high or your lowest low self. At first, you might have thought you could control these mood swings, and it's because you were still strong-willed then.

However, you soon realize that control is relative: you keep chasing the dragon, you chase the high for survival, not recognizing that you are losing a battle that should first be won in the mind. And the mind is a facet, a part of the soul. The soul is made up of willpower, the mind, and emotions. Then one realizes that drugs are a weapon formed against and made to infiltrate the soul to affect your true self; the inner man – the spirit being you are.

Drugs are made to manipulate your thought process: to establish images and beliefs using your imagination, and for your emotions to alter your willpower. And all this gravitates to an undesirable life experience. I have come to know Someone Who lives in me now, Whom we will later reveal. The One Who knows these things, and it's His pleasure to reveal and teach you these things also.

Note: This book contains some words and phrases that might seem unnecessary and repetitive. These are intentionally added to help drive the focus on the subject's intent.

"My people are destroyed for lack of knowledge:" - Hosea 4:6 KJV

And this is a rippling effect in our lives. In our careers, commerce, health, psyche, and relationships. For instance, the difference between the wealthy and the poor is that the first know something that the latter doesn't, thus the poor suffers economic disparities. In my high school year, a senior pupil poisoned himself and died because his well-off parents didn't want to buy him a silk suit for his matric farewell. His mindset was that of either my way (which was limited) or no way. He could not see other possibilities around his life manifesting into a greater reality than what he could fathom because of peer pressure. Back then a silk suit was the in-thing, today it's not. Fashion evolves all the time, when you know this, your life will not revolve around clothing items. The same goes for a person who understands that poverty is a mindset, it is a place, and when you realize it, you can choose to move out and find out about the place you want to live at. Find out about the how-tos of life and work towards achieving that.

Wisdom *is* truly the principal thing to acquire. Understanding will keep you in all your ways.

I can identify with and know that it is a complicated condition to be hooked on drugs. Most people start as a fun thing or experimenting, but they end up miserable from undesirable situations and experiences. Only the word of God can switch on the light inside of you, show you, reveal to you, and equip you with the power to rule again. You are not your circumstances!

"And ye shall know the truth, and the truth shall make you free." - *John 8:32 KJV*

Facts are different from truths, and facts are not truths. Facts are subject to change, they are only temporal landmarks, they are temporal guidelines to an ongoing ever-changing process. The truth remains and is not bound by time or space. The facts of your circumstances might dictate and seem realistic even that you are a drug addict and your future seems dim, but this is not the truth about you when you find out about the grand scheme (you as a finished product, you as a divinely created being with a purpose) of who you really and truthfully are. Have you ever seen an old car stripped down and in the process of being refurbished? You wouldn't show it to your lady friend and promise her a date ride in it. But when it's all kitted out, you'll surely have the confidence to say hey let's go out for a drink. What you knew and could comprehend when you were ten years old doesn't necessarily matter now, except in most cases it's those aspirations that still count. The same applies to what your current circumstance is, it will not matter in the next ten years should you choose life instead of death.

Some individuals don't know who they are, what they are made of, and what their purpose in life is. The above scripture states that (and it's only when you dig in the scriptures to find out and fully know) you shall "<u>know the truth</u>", this is a special type of knowing, a divine knowledge: it is a force, it is a revelation type knowledge (an awareness, awe, a disclosure), the type that you don't forget because it becomes part of you when you get it. It is an impartation of force-carrying information (building block) straight to your spirit man (for awareness) then to your soul (for remembrance, to re-member, to put together), where your mind is (which is a facet of the soul). Hence you will know, believe, and have faith in things the eye can hardly see. Not the other way around where we understand something by processing it in our minds and then accepting it in our hearts (spirit man). You might say that everything has to go through the mind first for processing! Not always. You move your limbs more often without mind processes. It is an example of your spirit willing on the body (spirit –> soul –> body-> impacting environment: living from inside out). This knowing is life-changing power revealed and attached to the real you – being equipped, being built. And "…the truth" (which shall make you free) is the word of God; which is the divine dynamic power of God encapsulated in text for your benefit, which is the scriptures (2 Timothy 3:14-17), of which when you meditate on (studying and constantly thinking of, and to utter, to speak out loud to yourself to store in your heart and to do) will make you free. You become those words, you become what those words say you are.

"This Book of the Law shall not depart out of your mouth, but you shall meditate on it day and night, that you may observe and do according to all that is written in it. For then you shall make your way prosperous, and then you shall deal wisely and have good success." - Joshua 1:8 AMP

Note the above: it says "you" (not God, not parents, not brother nor sister, or anybody else) shall make your own way prosperous, deal wisely, and have good success. The Word makes, equips, and builds you. And you make and build your own way. These attributes are a result of an individual having a certain level of information in them. When you study further you realize who the word of God is, which is the mystery of the person of Jesus Christ. And the word became flesh! So is the arrangement with you.

8

"I am the way, the truth, and the life:" - John 14:6 KJV

Jesus didn't say - I am "a" way, "a" truth, or "a" life, which might depict some different types of ways, truths, or lives: but used a definite article "the" way, "the" truth and "the" life. So, the exact path of life itself that you seek, is Him.

"And I will ask the Father, and He will give you another Comforter (Counselor, Helper, Intercessor, Advocate, Strengthener, and Standby), that He may remain with you forever- The Spirit of Truth, Whom the world cannot receive (welcome, take to its heart), because it does not see Him or know and recognize Him. But you know and recognize Him, for He lives with you [constantly] and will be in you." - John 14:16-17 AMP

*"And now, brethren, I commend you to God, and to the word of His grace, which is **able** to build you up, and to give you an __inheritance__ among all them which are sanctified." - Acts 20:32 KJV*
And now [brethren], I commit you to God [I deposit you in His charge, entrusting you to His protection and care]. And I commend you to the Word of His grace [to the commands and counsels and promises of His unmerited favor]. It is able to build you up and to give you [your rightful] inheritance among all God's set-apart ones (those consecrated, purified, and transformed of soul)." - Acts 20:32 AMP

Notice also in the above scripture, the freely given benefits (unmerited favor) are for those who are purified and transformed; meaning they were once not clean, and now are clean by the acknowledgment of the commands and counsels and promises of God and are thus continually being built and transformed in their mind, will and emotions (soul). God doesn't seek to save the self-righteous, those who perceive they don't need help or can do it by their willpower, but those who cry out needy to Him even when unclean in His sight.

"And be renewed in the spirit of your mind;" - Ephesians 4:23 KJV

Be rehabilitated in the character and strength of your soul (including intellect). I love God you know, this is one of the pieces of evidence we have around the world today showing His love and fairness to us all, even if you didn't have the opportunity for academics when you have Him you still make it and shine even brighter. All you require is being able to hear, read, and speak the word. There are numerous cases out there justifying this truth.

"But now thus saith the Lord that created thee, O Jacob **[Put Your Name]***, and He that formed thee, O Israel* **[Put Your Name]***, Fear not: for I have redeemed thee, I have called thee by thy name; thou art mine. When thou passest through the waters, I will be with thee; and through the rivers, they shall not overflow thee: when thou walkest through the fire, thou shalt not be burned; neither shall the flame kindle upon thee. For I am the Lord thy God, the Holy One of Israel, thy Saviour:"* - Isaiah 43:1-3 KJV

This is what The Creator, your Father Himself promises you about your life's journey. There is nothing to fear, no matter what you see or feel working against you. Hence I said facts are not truths. Do not be deterred by false circumstantial evidence, it is but a fleeting moment. If you don't give in, you will come to a remembrance of that which is but an illusion. God is the Creator of destinies and can rearrange destinies also. Jacob the swindler was redeemed to Israel the chosen nation. Position yourself for success!

"And be not conformed to this world: but be ye transformed by the renewing of your mind, that ye may prove what is that good, and acceptable, and perfect, will of God." - Romans 12:2 KJV

The world's systems and principles are nothing like God's ways of doing things; hence He says do not accept and do not play the game by worldly rules, because if you do, you are bound to lose, choose to renew your mind by learning His ways: And live your life with a different set of rules, you will surely win!

"Wherefore lay apart all filthiness and superfluity of naughtiness, and receive with meekness the engrafted word, which is able to save your souls." - James 1:21 KJV
"If we confess our sins, He is faithful and just to forgive us our sins, and to cleanse us from all unrighteousness." - 1 John 1:9 KJV

"But let patience have her perfect work, that ye may be perfect and entire, wanting nothing." - James 1:4 KJV

"And God is able to make all grace (every favor and earthly blessing) come to you in abundance, so that you may always and under all circumstances and whatever the need be self-sufficient [possessing enough to require no aid or support and furnished in abundance for every good work and charitable donation]." – 2 Corinthians 9:8 AMP

"But seek ye first the kingdom of God, and his righteousness; and all these things shall be added unto you. Take therefore no thought for the morrow: for the morrow shall take thought for the things of itself. Sufficient unto the day is the evil thereof." - Matthew 6:33-34 KJV

"If God gives such attention to the appearance of wildflowers-most of which are never seen—don't you think he'll attend to you, take pride in you, do his best for you? What I'm trying to do here is to get you to relax, to not be so preoccupied with getting, so you can respond to God's giving. People who don't know God and the way he works fuss over these things, but you know both God and how he works. Steep your life in God-reality, God-initiative, God-provisions. Don't worry about missing out. You'll find all your everyday human concerns will be met.

Give your entire attention to what God is doing right now, and don't get worked up about what may or may not happen tomorrow. God will help you deal with whatever hard things come up when the time comes." - Matthew 6:30-34 MSG

"My son, attend to my words; consent and submit to my sayings. Let them not depart from your sight; keep them in the center of your heart. For they are life to those who find them, healing and health to all their flesh." - Proverbs 4:20-22 AMP

"Above all else, guard your affections. For they influence everything else in your life." - Proverbs 4:23 Living Bible (TLB)

The question is what have you accustomed yourself to be affectionate about? Some people love to be miserable; they like to hurt others because they are hurt, and they don't see why others around them should be happy while they are not. This impacts and influences their lives negatively, no one wants to be around them and everything about them is unfulfilling. While others on the other hand are just favored in every way imaginable, and this is because what they are affectionate about, what they keep in their hearts has to do with love, peace, and joy.

When you wake up being morbid and unpleasant even to yourself, to the point where you even feel sorry for yourself, feeling victimized, your day will be unproductive and all else is influenced by your condition. Also, should I be affectionate and very pleasant to my wife on a day, she responds appropriately and so does everyone else in the house and elsewhere. However, should I get into a fight with her, I might end up sleeping on the couch. But mastery of your emotions leads to a peaceable life.

"Wherefore gird up the loins of your mind, be sober, and hope to the end for the grace that is to be brought unto you at the revelation of Jesus Christ;" - 1 Peter 1:13 KJV

CHAPTER 2

The Contract You Entered Into: Verbal and Intent

"For by thy words thou shalt be justified, and by thy words thou shalt be condemned." – *Matthew 12:37*

Anything you are constantly thinking of, imagining, and speaking of, becomes an overwhelming presence in your life. It manifests and crystallizes into this plane in your natural life. What you say is right – be it good or not.

Those who use drugs can attest to experiencing an upset stomach just before fetching a delivery of cocaine. This doesn't necessarily happen to first-time users, but if one's body is so accustomed to drugs that it expels all essential nutrients just before a hit, suggests a very sinister notion. Something has taken dominion over the body and the well-being of your domain. When you consider taking a laxative, for example, your stomach doesn't churn; you must wait a while after taking the laxative before it takes effect. But just the thought of that line up your nose discharges all minerals and strength from the body and readies the door wide open for devilish activity.

What does this mean? I have pondered and tried to understand the concept that most have contemplated in worry when confusion strikes – "selling one's soul to the devil." This can be tormenting and confounding to drug users who are genuinely concerned about their well-being, especially spiritually. This often happens after sleepless nights when you are strained in spirit, soul, and body. I however concluded that all creation belongs to God; you can never sell what is not yours. You are only in charge and accountable. The devil only sells you lies, as a con artist would.

With reflection, you realize that you have been excessively praising drugs and that your dependence on them has become problematic, and now binding, despite the negative impact they have had on your life. It has dawned on you how miserable you have become. Some people create idols and shrines for worship, but it is not the objects themselves that are worshiped, but rather a specific demon associated with that object that is being summoned for favors or sacrifices. Similarly, spirits cannot successfully affect the physical realm without a physical host, and neither can they possess someone without their consent. God Himself cannot act in one's life or send His Holy Spirit to dwell in them without their permission. Both the natural and the spiritual realms are governed by their laws and principles. And here is the one-way traffic to an abyss below;

"They are doomed and their fate is eternal misery (perdition); their god is their stomach (their appetites, their sensuality) and they glory in their shame, siding with earthly things and being of their party." - Philippians 3:19 AMP

There is a mystery to life, and we will try to explore and uncover this later. It's important to note that spirit beings are not bound by death, they do not die, and life does not reside solely in the flesh. The scripture states that those who align themselves with the fleshly nature are destined to condemnation and will face eternal anguish, while those who are spiritually minded in the Lord are blessed and experience eternal life in the presence of God.

Just as the first Adam did, by choosing to act and be deceived by Lucifer's schemes, you are giving up control of your mind and allowing yourself to be controlled. This is spiritual dethronement. You relinquish your own power and authority, handing it over to another being. You are handing over your kingship. The rulers of the fallen world are deceptive, and Lucifer is the father of all lies. Be careful to not get mangled in an arena you have no mastery in.

Here's how he works:

He capitalizes on human emotions driven by imagination – he aims to get you as emotional as possible, drugs or not. Hence, from the time you consume drugs, it always leads to and ends up being an endless emotional roller coaster caused by a bombardment of thoughts. This one friend would say, "I'm racing, I'm at a million revs per second" – thoughts. These are waters of unrest. You get too in tune with your emotions. Logic gets clouded as a result. Recognize that reason, the process leading to logic, is from the mind which is part of the soul. You can see, even when you are coming down from the high, that every little issue in your life is blown out of proportion – emotion driven. When you lose the battle in your mind – when you can't reconcile reason and are not headstrong, you resort to what you have accustomed yourself to, which is the next best feeling. And those feelings are tracked to what you expect from another line of cocaine – emotions driving the willpower: dictating to the conscious mind what is acceptable to think and to live by. But the inevitable is that these track of thoughts evolve into a mindset. As a man thinks in his heart, so is he. You become what your negative trail of thoughts has dictated you are, and what you believe becomes true. Belief systems are created. Then your outlook on life is perceived as to what the devil has sold you. At this point, it is clear who the puppet master is. This is called *hustling*; get someone in the game, make it appear as if he or she is winning and feeling good for a while, and then take it all. Nevertheless, we are responsible and accountable for our choices, conscious or not, and where they may lead us.

"So then those who are living the life of the flesh [catering to the appetite and impulses of their carnal nature] cannot please or satisfy God, or be acceptable to Him." - Romans 8:8 AMP

"So kill (deaden, deprive of power) the evil desire lurking in your members [those animal impulses and all that is earthly in you that is employed in sin]: sexual vice, impurity, sensual appetites, unholy desires, and all greed and covetousness, for that is idolatry (the deifying of self and other created things instead of God)." - Colossians 3:5 AMP

Take note of what God is saying about the latter, that you should deprive of power the evil desire lurking in your body – this means it's our responsibility to actively work towards depriving the evil forces of power within us, which came from the above-described attributes of laboring in sin. It also implies that it was a conscious choice to allow these forces in, and it is also a conscious choice to take action to remove them.

Who have you agreed from within to worship or deify?

Some things in life are very subtle. Have you ever taken notice of gestures and mannerisms every time you take drugs? Let alone the praising of the substance, how good it is, what an experience you have when you hit, you actually *bow* when you take drugs. And you do this every day, like a religious rite with adoration and devotion?

Since the beginning of time, we have known humanity falling short of glory because of idol deifying. God created us and put everything else under us. He is a jealous God. He gets upset when humans practice idolatry and are controlled by the very things that were made to serve them. He loves you more than you could ever imagine - you are His own. No parent would desire for their child to be misled or be under any sort of bondage.

Everything was put under man, yet we see not everything else yet under the feet of man, but we see Jesus. *Ref. - Hebrews 2:8-9 KJV*

He is our hope of victory.

CHAPTER 3
Your World View As An Addict

The way you perceive the world around you moment by moment gives you a view and an experience of life on earth. This is only from what you are conscious of at any given moment, not what you know or do not, due to forgetfulness. Even sober people function on autopilot for most of their days. i.e. When you are about to go out of your house to drive to the shops, you do not consciously put the thought of opening your house door at the forefront of your brain, you could also be talking on your cell phone while you open the door and get to the car to find that you have forgotten your wallet in the house. Generally, you don't forget to take your wallet when you are about to drive out; it is because you consciously choose to think about it at that moment, you broadcast the thought consciously and would not have to experience the brief frustration of returning from the shops. Yes, unconsciousness can lead to brief or prolonged frustrations in our life experiences. And this is a choice made by one to live a life of practicing to be aware of things, not just living an I wouldn't be bothered type of lifestyle.

Knowledge, choices, and focus are integral and vital components of our daily routine. If any of these are impaired, it is likely to lead to flawed or poor outcomes that can have a cascading effect on future events in one's life.

As a drug addict, one experiences a life of ongoing distress, pressure, and a clouded mental state. Mood swings are frequent and difficult to manage due to an inner persistent sense of oppression and self-condemnation. The ability to think clearly and make sound decisions is hindered. Your brain activity is consistently elevated, and most of the thoughts that you conceive and accept have a subtle negative predisposition. One sees life through a twisted lens, and problems are left to fester and be.

These thoughts are repetitive and are stored in your subconscious, and this is the automated engine, what we call second nature: what's stored in here happens even when you don't notice - as not forgetting to breathe or remembering to walk. When your body finally gets rest, your subconscious reinstates all that it has been told repeatedly as facts and makes them *truths*. All this material that gets established in your mind has a dark nature, hence all you see is gloom when you are not high. Then the need to stimulate the happy feeling comes again. But what most users don't realize is that they are practicing self-reliance on emotions, worshiping drugs as a savior, and feelings get the better of them. They are sense ruled! Even in business, it's not safe to make emotional decisions. Emotions are good, they are there for us to enjoy, like any good sweet thing out there to eat, however, the more you do it recklessly, it will kill you. You ought to control your feelings, not the other way around.

We know that the mind is a battleground, and an idle mind is the devil's playground. So, when you are constantly high and coming down, who's winning, who's in charge? This is no joke, remember all that you feed (hearing, seeing, knowing, perceiving, deciding, and focusing) on, becomes your mindset. This determines your character and aura. And the aura you carry can attract or repel all else. Hence most addicts find themselves not knowing who they are anymore.

Let's explore one subtle yet powerful force you could ever harbor known as Fear, which is a feeling of unease or alarm triggered by the anticipation of danger or harm. It is the emotional response to the perception of threat. It is either to be afraid of someone or something. These are but a few words to describe the associations with fear. We all have memories of our early childhood years and the feelings associated with darkness and fear. Symbolically, we are sensitive to the significance of light and darkness and the effects thereof.

The key aspect to note from the above is the emotional response to the perceived energy. Fear can manifest in two ways; one is by thought process (induced thoughts from within culminating in possession), and the other by the sudden presence (fear-inhabited spirit) imposing to possess. And the design behind fear is for it to have a dwelling place in man, and we understand that behind every designer product, there is a deployment strategy.

Let's have a look at a strategy for deploying fear.

Thought process

Distract someone's focus to deter them from their belief and confidence in something, by introducing a lie or false idea that works against their preference or knowledge. This will cause doubt if the lie is bought for a considerable window period. You build on the lie by feeding more alternative linked scenarios, fitting and supporting facts regarding the first lie (ideology). This will give the first lie credence, and possibilities become endless on how factual that idea can be. Once this is established, it isn't a matter of true or false anymore, but a delve into a subject that doesn't need focus nor attention because its basis and merits are flawed and couldn't be true after all. However, many find themselves on a journey in their minds let alone practical life experiences which shouldn't have been. And once this has started, only pressure can follow. Pressure will create anxiety, anxiety creates panic, and panic creates a lack of focus leading to a lack of confidence leading to fear.

When fear is established, you think you can learn how to control it, and live by hiding it, manipulating every circumstance to suit perceptions and confidence, by hook or by crook.

Nevertheless, you are only influenced from within by these internal forces driving your actions by the power of suggestion. And it's these drivers that are in charge, not you. Hence you see such narcissism ruining relationships and people start seeing through you. You then are perceived as not trustworthy, and all that goes with that.

Fear is run by its laws - a code of a set standard of forces deployed for disruption by evil, if practiced well by someone, will lead to their destruction.

Consider, for instance, Samantha, a wonderful lady who is greatly admired by her loved ones, seen as a delight and a remarkable person to spend time with. An awesome girl that has much to offer. She walks into a crowded room at a party, and can't help but feel self-conscious, her eyes scanning the sea of faces for a familiar one. She feels like everyone is judging her, looking at her round stomach and her thick self. She had always struggled with her weight and is now fresh from a breakup with her boyfriend. Tonight is no different, the ex-boyfriend's words ringing in her ears, "when are you going to lose weight?" She can't stop thinking about how fat she must look in her dress, and how she doesn't belong among all these thin, beautiful people. She feels like an outsider, and it's all because of her weight. She doesn't want to be here anymore and just wants to go home and hide away from the judgmental eyes of others – meanwhile, not knowing, her beauty had struck David like a lightning bolt and left him enchanted off his feet.

Our bodies are different because of age, genetic constructs, race, and culture. There is always the right individual for everyone, the one who will worship the grounds you walk on.

By the point of thinking that she is fat, she could decide to acknowledge all the facts and truths about how pretty she looks and feels, especially in those outfits she bought for all those other occasions. How wonderful she felt on that particular day, and all the pleasing compliments she got, or, she can conceive the idea that she's fat and be on her way to unknown feelings which has nothing to do with her weight.

This idea has a lot to do with emotions and thoughts. "You are fat" to a well-built woman has to do with a sequence of misconceptions regarding certain circumstances. Could be from a broken relationship, or a promiscuous man leaving her for another infatuation with another woman. Not knowing the truth and being unable to discern the real cause, this woman will believe she is fat. Now, what she'll start realizing is facts from ideas built on the comparison. I wasn't this fat at that time, or, so and so is more beautiful than I am, or if I could be like that, I would feel better.

This is *self-doubt* in motion, and it will go on and on. But this has no truth about her. That lie, which was just an idea from somewhere (from the enemy) is conceived, and it's now causing doubt and evolving towards fear. What ifs and whatnots, the future of being confident and well-balanced starts having unknown dependencies, pressure builds up and this can be dreadful. At this point, fear gets established and can grow into a monster.

She then might attract that which is not good for her: i.e., drugs can make you lose weight and make you happy, another lie; like a man who just wants to use her, promises and more promises, then hooks her on drugs and attach a tag to her. Remember fear wants to have a place in you, deter you from confidence, control your thought process, and decision making to destroy you.

Sudden Presence of Fear

Fear can come suddenly (and it is always with a purpose) or can be in a specific environment till an individual goes to such a place and experience it (haunted places with evil presence). A dog suddenly barking at you can scare you (NB: Dogs are not evil). You can either develop an attitude and a mindset towards not being scared of dogs, and this can be achieved in many ways, or choose to be terrified by dogs to a point where you confess with your mouth that you are afraid of dogs. And trust me you will find that even when you see a Chihuahua, fear will rise from within. A sudden scene from a horror movie can startle and scare you. These types of films intend to generate fear in viewers, starting as a form of leisure, but then excessive exposure to scares may lead to an increase in fear.

You can be working on a project while sitting and pondering, you get a brilliant idea and you plan around it. However, suddenly you get and feel this sudden fear in your gut when you have to deploy or present your idea, then you begin to think of all the reasons why it's not such a good idea after all. This type of fear is to deter you from something good about to happen.

"Be not afraid of sudden fear, neither of the desolation of the wicked, when it cometh. For the Lord shall be thy confidence, and shall keep thy foot from being taken." - Proverbs 3:25-26 KJV

Fear is having faith in your adversary. Your adversary can be anything that works against you, to hinder your progress. When you are constantly afraid, you will believe to be inadequate and will embrace failure.

"In whom the god of this world hath blinded the minds of them which believe not, lest the light of the glorious gospel of Christ, who is the image of God, should shine unto them." - 2 Corinthians 4:4 KJV

Fear represents the absence of faith in a person. God has given all men a measure of faith. Hope and faith are intertwined. But what happens when you misuse your faith? Like anything else that gets misused, it fades away. There was a day when you used to dream of things working out for you. As an addict you find yourself with no dreams really, let alone you don't sleep. Routes are already set out, however, when you are on the wrong route and deterred from your destiny, no matter what you do, you will not get to your destination unless you retrace your steps and wear your proper gear toward the right route leading to your destination.

If you are in Pretoria and want to travel to Johannesburg, you have to get on to the N1 South, should you find yourself en route to the N1 North, you will end up in Limpopo, and you will never get to Johannesburg unless you gather more fuel and herd back on to N1 South to your destination which is Johannesburg.

Faith can be measured: this tells us it can increase or decrease and has stages. A person who doesn't dream is as good as a dead man walking, their faith is broken. And a broken faith will let you know that hope is gone. As an addict, an inspiration for hope is so short-lived that it gets swallowed by this dark cloud as quickly as it came. This is why people lose hope and faith in those struggling with addiction - due to the negative actions and emotions that often accompany addiction, such as fear, deceit, theft, anger, confusion, unreliability, and a lack of control over one's life. These negative influences can create self-doubt and a lack of direction and can lead to the absence of true joy.

Remember, we must highlight all dark and hidden areas, this material is not to condemn you, but to expose and rebuke the evil that has influenced and lied to you. Please read on.

CHAPTER 4
Your Current Self – Why Doesn't God Help Me?

God created boundaries for your protection as a loving parent would limit their child's movement because of what might hurt them ignorantly so. Kids must learn as they grow, and the willingness to know more capacitates potential. This is key.

Adam and Eve hid from God, and when God asked them where they were, Adam said they were hiding because they were naked. Fear had entered their lives, and it enters through sin. God asked them, "Who told you that you were naked?" God knew they had been fooled by the devil, and as a result, they fell from glory. Do you get the parallel? You were ok before drugs; you tasted, opened unsavory doors, got lied to, fear got the best of you, and you fell from glory. But do you know that God never cursed man (Adam or Eve)? He just asked Adam what happened, and Adam said it's the woman you gave me. I guess this was the beginning of excuses. And He asked Eve, and she said it was the serpent, and God never asked the serpent. He just cursed the devil and the ground for man's sake. The rest was a consequence of what He had warned them would happen when they ate of the fruit of the knowledge of good and evil.

Life as an addict is the life of a person with an infected code, like a computer infected with a virus. Negative thoughts and lies get engraved in your mind, and like a tape you keep playing those words over and over again, like a virus-infected machine, you will crash if not helped. Ultimately every area of your life has this unbelievable stream of failure. No matter what you do, things appear not to work for you. This seems like a *setup*. If a man's soul is shut down, you can't access his spirit. The soul is the doorway to a man's spirit. That's why sometimes you can't help people with deep-seated issues. Their souls are wounded so badly that whatever you try to say or do seems to be in vain. It's like you are hitting a brick wall.

"Hope deferred maketh the heart sick" – Proverbs 13:12

Let's take a look at the life of one of the greatest men of God: Job.

Job loved God, and he worshiped and served the Lord [fear of the Lord is translated from the original text meaning to worship and serve God reverently so. The devil has twisted the knowledge of the word of God over the years, and that is why people interpret the fear of God as being afraid of God which is false. Contrary to what God wants; this is an intimate relationship with Him. In any successful relationship, we understand there has to be love, and love is based on trust. Fear is the opposite end of trust].

Deuteronomy 6:13 says *"Thou shalt fear the LORD thy God, and serve him, and shalt swear by his name."*

But did you know that Jesus quoted this very passage, and interpreted it much differently?

In *Luke 4:8* *"And Jesus answered and said unto him, Get thee behind me, Satan: for it is written, Thou shalt worship the Lord thy God, and him only shalt thou serve."*

Fear and love cannot coexist.

1 John 4:18 says *"There is no fear in love; but perfect love casteth out fear: because fear hath torment. He that feareth is not made perfect in love."*

25

Knowing God's love for us (which we cannot know if we are afraid of Him) is crucial to our ability to experience the fullness of God in our lives. *"That Christ may dwell in your hearts by faith; that ye, being rooted and grounded in love, May be able to comprehend with all saints what is the breadth, and length, and depth, and height; And to know the love of Christ, which passeth knowledge, that ye might be filled with all the fulness of God." - Ephesians 3:17-19 KJV*

Now he (Job) was perfect and upright, and he steered clear away from evil. God had blessed him with absolutely all things a man could want, family, possessions, riches, wisdom, etc. One day as the angels came to present themselves to God, there came Satan also among them. God asked him where he was coming from. And Satan replied from going to and fro in the earth, and from walking up and down in it. Because this guy doesn't really have a home.

Nevertheless, God boasted about Job to him, asking him if he had seen His servant Job. That there is none like him on the earth, a perfect and upright man, one that serves and loves God and shunned evil.

Then Satan answered the Lord, and said, *"does not Job fear God for nothing? Has not God made a **hedge** around him, and around his house, and around all that he has on every side?"* Satan continued saying to God, *"You have blessed the work of his hands, and his substance is increased in the land. And he continued, but should you take away all that he has, he (Job) will surely curse You to the face."*

What happens to Job as you read from Job1:12 onwards is one of the biggest losses and a sad story a man can ever experience. Some people misinterpret that God had allowed the devil to attack Job and it is not so. A lot had happened as you read between *Job1 verse 11 into verse 12*; because verse 12 opens with God saying to Satan that;

"Behold- meaning Look, See!, all that he has is in your power, all else you can take but his life."

God said, "Look", addressing Satan because the "hedge" was now broken – some time had passed by. The hedge that God Himself had built for Job, the hedge that Satan couldn't penetrate to attack Job. This tells us something: Satan couldn't break it, God built it, and surely God couldn't have broken it. So someone else had broken the hedge.

As you study this book of Job, as much blessed as he was, there was this element of fear he entertained. Let's look at this in – Job 1:5

"And it was so, when the days of their feasting were gone about, that Job sent and sanctified them, and rose up early in the morning, and offered burnt offerings according to the number of them all (his children): for Job said, It may be that my sons have sinned, and cursed God in their hearts. Thus did Job continually."

Job forgot who had blessed him in all his success. Why would God bless you and take it away? This is not consistent with His nature. Job had entertained much fear in his fruitful life.

In *Job 1:21 he says "Naked came I out of my mother's womb, and naked shall I return thither: the Lord gave, and the Lord hath taken away; blessed be the name of the Lord."* Job's thinking here was flawed. *Verse 22 says "In all this Job sinned not, nor charged God foolishly."*

We see evidence of this fear in the third chapter when he says: *"For the thing which I greatly feared is come upon me, and that which I was afraid of is come unto me. I was not in safety, neither had I rest, neither was I quiet; yet trouble came."* - *Job3:25-26*

Neither was I quiet? This means he constantly professed his fears. Job went everywhere talking about his fears as if when you talk about your fears you will prevent them from happening (you attract that which you constantly think and speak about). Job went about confessing the wrong things. What we constantly speak comes to light. He never rested; he was constantly making sacrifices to God just in case one of his sons might have sinned – this is doubt. The man was loved so much by God but he could not discern even his safety; that hedge Satan couldn't penetrate. Trouble was bound to come because he was the one that broke the hedge.

"He that diggeth a pit shall fall into it; and whoso breaketh an hedge, a serpent shall bite him." - Ecclesiastes 10:8 KJV
"Surely the serpent will bite without enchantment; and a babbler is no better." - Ecclesiastes 10:11 KJV

Job opened a spiritual door letting serpents (demons, evil spirits) into his life. And the serpent surely bit. This reveals to us how Satan uses his devices to gain access to our lives. We must guard ourselves against opening doors to the enemy. Defilement is the number one door to demonic bondage. Paul was well aware of this in *2 Corinthians 2:11 "Lest Satan should get an advantage of us: for we are not ignorant of his devices."* As we have seen in the book of Job, there is a hedge (spiritual wall) of protection that surrounds God's people, but if we punch a hole in that hedge, it is an open door to the enemy and we can get bitten by evil spirits (serpents). Defilement (meaning unclean or polluted) causes these doors to be opened. If you cut your skin and let it get dirty (defiled), it would make you vulnerable to infection. The same happens in the spiritual realm, except the gems in this case are unclean spirits.

So with drugs you have defiled yourself and broken the hedge, you have dug a pit; you have punched holes in your wall of protection. The doors are wide open for unclean spirits to enter your life to infect, defile, and affect all areas even those you come across to be influenced. It's a chain reaction and these are the devil's devices. That's how he gains an advantage over your life. But like Job, even when he was on the brink of destruction, all was not hopeless. God stepped in, He always does, and He will step in to spank you just like your natural parent would. He loves you, He will correct you even if He has to be harsh. But it is your choice to stick it through the harsh words. it's worth it.

"My son, do not despise or shrink from the chastening of the Lord [His correction by punishment or by subjection to suffering or trial]; neither be weary of or impatient about or loath or abhor His reproof, For whom the Lord loves He corrects, even as a father corrects the son in whom he delights." Proverbs 3:11-12 AMPC

God intervened with Job also, He had to deal with him, even his spiritual pride [which most of God's children tend to fall short of *("Every one that is proud in heart is an abomination to the Lord: though hand join in hand, he shall not be unpunished" - Proverbs 16:5 KJV)*]; Job thought he knew it all. But God came and chastised him and showed him where he was wrong (Job heeded the voice of God), and then God blessed him even more than he had lost. Allow God to deal with you also. What's impossible with man is possible with God. Don't be all-knowing. All of creation is His, He knows better. It is His pleasure for you to find out much of these mysteries and become a better and more excellent human. Train yourself to be obedient then you will succeed in all your endeavors.
"But whoso hearkeneth unto me shall dwell safely, and shall be quiet from fear of evil - harm." - Proverbs 1:33 KJV

CHAPTER 5
The Natural and The Supernatural

The Natural

We can define the natural world as the manifestation of matter in this biosphere, even in the universe, the tangible material we live in and around, visible to the naked eye.

Our conscious awareness lets us perceive the world we live in as reality. This physical world for some people is a world whereby all in it exists independently, and from which all other things in its entirety are derived. This should then mean: cause and effect on this plane of existence are encapsulated and therefore devoid of influence from anywhere else outside this perceived reality. If I should create anything, resolve a problem or issue in this material world, I have to create something new with what's already here, or, investigate the symptoms to lead me to the root cause, and then I would understand how to get to the solution only within this plane of existence.

All things visible are evident and can be tangible.

When a person is involved in a car accident, for instance, they might succumb to physical injury to their body. The solution to this is that the physicians would examine the injuries, treat the wounds, then prescribe medication to ease pain and help with any other ailment.

So the illness, in this case, is more physically oriented, being resolved with physical solutions. The medical field treats illnesses and cures people from infectious viruses and diseases of all sorts. These viruses as small as they are, are only visible to the naked eye using specialized equipment. Therefore, it is not only those things that we can readily see with the naked eye that we can reasonably say influence and affects us and is part of this physical world, then label them as real.

Science accounts for the sub-atomic properties of matter, which is condensed energy, which the eye cannot see, like an atom, formed by molecules, formed by particles. And we know other things exist in this plane we call reality or the natural. Things like words spoken, as intangible as they are, are sound. Science can prove the wavelength and the type of wave they produce. Words have cause and effect on humanity and they are part of our existence.

The mind, the will, and the emotions; we all have them, but they are intangible and we all depend on them. You can dream (seeing with your eyes shut) and then wake up feeling connected to what you were seeing, that it felt real as intangible as the dream was. So how can something that never existed come to manifest into this plane we call reality - which is encapsulated and devoid of influence from without? We understand that nature dictates things appear from somewhere, into the physical, and from growing small to big then succumbing to decay out of this plane.

Biological studies explain relatively well the conception of human life in the womb and the growth thereof, but consciousness as familiar as it is, its inception and disposition are still puzzling to studies and haven't been figured out yet. Neither has the big bang theory provided sufficient proof about the origin of the universe per se and is slowly being rejected in cosmological studies. Besides, physicists tell us that the mathematics behind the string theory suggests multiple dimensions of existence (multiverses) to reconcile and unify general relativity (the law of gravitation and its relation to other forces of nature) and the quantum world, of which these two theories on their own cannot agree, apart of the string theory, then science is stuck. We could then could ask, how far the boundary of the universe is if such exists since we are told it is still expanding. Or how far small can we go beyond the condensed energy that is said to give everything its mass, the Higgs boson, to accept the borderline of particles to call them real? So which dimension do these small particles exist in? Is it the fourth, fifth, or simply just a parallel world? Is it correct to call this parallel world a dimension? Stars collapse on themselves through nuclear fusion, like a powerful stellar explosion of a supernova creating a black hole. What's beyond it? Is gravity self-existent, or a byproduct of the Higgs field? Is it possible to know and explain it all?

On the contrary, theologians have been quite satisfied thus far with their conviction and understanding of multiple dimensions of existence, even the third heaven, a realm beyond this physical universe as Paul had said in 2 Corinthians 12:2.

The physical natural world is not independent and without influence from without, it is highly dependent and governed by the spirit realm. As discussed, particle physics enlightens that the main building blocks of all matter at the sub-atomic level are the elementary particles called fermions, which are a class of quarks and leptons. An electron particle has a pair partner particle, an antielectron or a positron, the same weight, and the same spin, but opposite charge. Just as all these small particles (up quarks, down quarks, charm quarks, strange quarks, top quarks, bottom quarks, muons, tauons, etc) have antiparticle pairs, when they collide at high energy, they annihilate each other and form energy or another particle (e.g. composite particle – proton) in another field, molecule, matter, or antimatter. The mystery however is, modern science has deduced that the evolution of the universe has favored the creation of matter particles over antimatter particles in creation. Meaning, when particles collided, celestial and terrestrial bodies as matter were formed, and more antimatter particles are unaccounted for.

I'm saying all this to indicate that we are light beings occupying matter in its condensed state – a very low frequency of existence. Similarly, there should be energy in its pure form - a higher frequency of existence.

The Supernatural

The supernatural is generally perceived as non-existent and often spoken of as folklore, the stuff of mysticism. Some do think it does exist but has nothing to do with us. It is just fairy tales for some people, and when human nature doesn't understand something, we tend to ridicule such notions if not making utter nonsensical apprehension in misconceptions – mistaken beliefs.

"Who is this that questions my wisdom with such ignorant words? Brace yourself like a man, because I have some questions for you, and you must answer them.
Where were you when I laid the foundations of the earth? Tell me, if you know so much. Who determined its dimensions and stretched out the surveying line?
Can you direct the movement of the stars – binding the cluster of the Pleiades or loosening the cords of Orion? Can you direct the constellations through the seasons or guide the Bear with her cubs across the heavens? Do you know the laws of the universe? Can you use them to regulate the earth? Who gives intuition to the heart and instinct to the mind?" – Job 38:2-3, 4-5, 31-33, 36 NLT
"And whosoever speaketh a word against the Son of man, it shall be forgiven him: but whosoever speaketh against the Holy Ghost, it shall not be forgiven him, neither in this world, neither in the world to come." – Matthew 12:32 KJV

The knowledge of divination and astrology using the constellations came to man through the fallen angels as described in the book of Enoch which we'll touch a bit on below. But how can you not be forgiven in a world to come if you die in this world? It is because we are spirit beings who continue to live after physical death, and the severity of the judgment of blasphemy against the Holy Ghost it's because He is the Will and Doer of God's work, the Creator Himself - Proverbs 8:22-31. To put it mildly, if you say He doesn't exist, you wouldn't exist. If you outrightly disobey your parents you might get kicked out of the house for good.

"And there was a woman there who for eighteen years had had an infirmity caused by a spirit (a demon of sickness). She was bent completely forward and utterly unable to straighten herself up or look upward. And when Jesus saw her, He called [her to Him] and said to her, Woman, you are released from your infirmity! Then He laid [His] hands on her, and instantly she was made straight, and she recognized and thanked and praised God." - Luke 13:11-13 AMP

This woman had been sick for eighteen years, and the cause of her illness was a demon of sickness. This on its own communicates to us that there are different types of demons, which are entities that operate from the spirit realm. Jesus "said" to her, "you are released from your sickness!". Scripture expresses to us that words are creating power (ref: Mark 11:23). With authority over the demon, Jesus released the woman from her bondage by speaking and releasing divine healing power from God and by laying of hands, then her spine was immediately straightened.

"The miraculous signs will accompany those who believe: They will cast out demons in my name, and they will speak in new languages. They will be able to place their hands on the sick, and they will be healed." – Mark 16:17-18 NLT

It is God's power (dunamis) affecting the physical by His "spoken" Word – Rhema.

Jesus was a man of flesh and blood when He walked on earth, and He said the things (miracles and healing) He did, were through the power of His Father Who was in Him - The Holy Spirit. He further indicated that when we receive the Holy Spirit which was yet to come by then after His ascension, we would do the same things He did, even more than He demonstrated.

There are replete illustrations in scripture where we get to understand the interaction, function, and effects the spirit world has on the physical world and the existence thereof.

Diverse nations around the world have different belief systems leading to specific worshiping of that which they have faith in. Be it worshiping of ancestors, Buddha, Satan, Scientology, or some form of entity perceived to be godlike and being a final destination to getting understanding, help, relief, or assistance, and this being an out-of-this-world power to appeal to, and to appease that there may be changes in their lives, be it positive or negative. [Ref. Isaiah 65:1-7(about familiar spirits)] These are spirit beings, and applying faith and works in those spirits in a particular realm is what causes an effect in the physical, not just believing. The difference is knowing what you are dealing with, its origin, its intent, and the consequence thereof. James 2:19 tells that even demons believe and tremble, but faith without works is dead.

Acting on the faith of what you believe in is the spiritual currency that causes changes in the natural. The only challenge is where the result is directed to, whether what you seek will take effect or not, this depends also on your understanding of the principles governing the spiritual. Should we not have God in our lives or fall short of His glory, we get overwhelmed by circumstances, and we then search for help from place to place. The aid beyond the sciences that is often perceived to work is from some observable ritual, believing that power comes from religious rites, charms, or potions. This is why the enemy has sought to lure people in by teaching them the dark arts since the fall of the messengers (The fallen angels) over many centuries.

"In those days, and for some time after, giant Nephilites lived on the earth, for whenever the sons of God [(fallen angels)] had intercourse with women, they gave birth to children who became the heroes and famous warriors of ancient times." – Genesis 6:4 NLT

Once upon a time someone dear to me casually said there isn't a thing that is named and doesn't exist, rather it's the broken telephone that distorts the description or event. Yes, we've always heard about demigods, try following the real story of the statue of the woman riding on the back of a bull in Europe and see where it leads you. – Revelations 17

The boof of Enoch (Hanok) describes the two hundred fallen angels:

"2 And the messengers, the children of the shamayim [heaven], saw and lusted after them, and said to one another: "Come, let us choose us wives from among the children of men and bring forth children."

3 And Shemyatsa, who was their leader, said unto them, "I fear you will not indeed agree to do this deed, and I alone shall have to pay the penalty of a great sin." 4 And they all answered him and said, "Let us all swear an oath, and all bind ourselves by mutual curses not to abandon this plan but to do this matter." 5 Then they all swore together and bound themselves by mutual curses upon it. 6 And they were, in all, two hundred who descended in the days of Yered on the summit of Mount Hermon, and they called it Mount Hermon because they had sworn and bound themselves by mutual curses upon it. 7 And these are the names of their leaders: Shamlatsats, their leader, Arakleba, Rame'ĕl, Kokab'ĕl, Tamle'ĕl, Ramle'ĕl, Dani'ĕl, Yehezqĕl, Baraki'ĕl, Asah'ĕl, Armaros, Batar'ĕl, Anan'ĕl, Tsaqle'ĕl, Shemshaphe'ĕl, Satar'ĕl, Tsuri'ĕl, Yomya'ĕl, Sari'ĕl. 8 These are their chiefs of tens.

And all the others together with them took unto themselves wives, and each chose one for himself, and they began to go in unto them and to defile themselves with them, 2 and they taught them charms and enchantments, and the cutting of roots, and made them to know plants. And they became pregnant, and they brought forth great giants, whose height was three thousand els: (approx. 137 meters tall)

Shemyatsa taught enchantments, and root cuttings, Armaros - the resolving of enchantments, Baraki'ĕl - astrology, Kokab'ĕl - the constellations, Yehezqĕl - the knowledge of the clouds, Araqi'ĕl - the signs of the earth, Shamsi'ĕl – the signs of the sun, and Sari'ĕl – the course of the moon." – Hanok 6:2-8, 7:1-2, 8:2

"But there was a certain man, called Simon, which before time in the same city used sorcery, and bewitched the people of Samaria, giving out that himself was some great one:" – *Acts 8:9*

Witchcraft exists and it works, as much as pharmaceutical treatment works. Pharmaceutical comes from the Greek word pharmakeia which means sorcery, the practice that arises from the understanding of contorting different plants, animal and human body parts, blood, water, and marine spirits to give life to demons to affect people and circumstances. But the power behind this ability is only temporal and doesn't last, hence those who practice this have to renew their charms periodically. But don't be fooled, this can only successfully work against you if you are not hedged in by the power of God.

You should know how to notice a deceptive demonic vision or dream if it's significant. You will notice that these entities can't hold form for long, they will try and mimic someone or something that you know. In the dream, for instance, you know you are interacting with say Peter, but it doesn't look like Peter for long as you focus, something is always amiss or displaced about it. Hence such dreams are never clear and a bit confusing, people just take the gist and underlying message and want to run with it. When God talks to you, nothing is confusing about it, it is clear as day. You will see and remember with clarity. Think about this for a second, God created these creatures that revealed this forbidden knowledge at the time. Why would you want to be under their clutches, rather than with God? As just an interesting fact, in the Book of Enoch, these fallen angels ask and send Enoch to plead with God on their behalf so that He may forgive them. But God tells Enoch that they (angels) ought to speak on behalf of man, and not a man to plead on behalf of angels. They would not be allowed back into heaven, and when their offspring (Nephilim) die, their spirits cannot return to God because they are not His, but are foul spirits bound to hell – resident evil. Not all fallen angels are bound in the abyss, just like Lucifer is still roaming like a lion looking for whomever he can devour, so as the disembodied Nephilim spirits cause havoc around the world. In isiZulu, there is a creature called umkhovu, which is an offspring of a human and a baboon (ape), which is used for witchcraft. Now tell me what kind of spirit will such an entity be when it dies? These are mischievous spirits like poltergeists. There is nothing new under the sun, and I think it's just best to use logic when information comes. The devil doesn't want people to open and study the bible to learn the truth, but they should be blinded and focus on tangible magic – to believe and trust only in things that can be physically seen.

Drug addiction is one form of slavery, and all forms of slavery are to oppress a particular group in society. When you are under the establishment of a tyrant, you will feed that kingdom and be devoid of any rights for your livelihood and well-being. But humans were not made to be oppressed, there is an entity that influences a man to oppress another because it is envious of the created human.

These are spiritual beings of the dark world, rulers of darkness. Nevertheless, they have certain powers but lost all authority. We through Christ Jesus have power and authority, which we'll discuss later on.

There are a lot of oppressive systems in some governments engineered to impact and destroy man in this world. These are footprints of hauntings of the same kind of decree. This order is present, prevalent, and surely out to get mankind. Give people all good and suitable conditions, then they will function under perfect love even for a stranger. However, in these latter days, these systems are crafted more subtly, to a mere person it would seem they are conspiracy theories. So if mankind is designed with such love in his core, but living contrary to his purpose, lets us deduce that he is influenced, and that influence has been having much power over him.

A human being is a free-will agent and is designed after the likeness of God.

"And God said, Let us make man in our image, after our likeness:" - Genesis 1:26 KJV
Man is spirit as God is Spirit;

"Furthermore we have had fathers of our flesh which corrected us, and we gave them reverence: shall we not much rather be in subjection unto the Father of spirits, and live?" – Hebrews 12:9

Our Creator is the Heavenly Father Himself, so we understand who our Master is. In the same breath should we choose from the gift of free-will to step out of the Master's will, we fall into the other world and the ruler thereof.

"No man can serve two masters: for either he will hate the one, and love the other; or else he will hold to the one, and despise the other. Ye cannot serve God and mammon." - Matthew 6:24 KJV
Now that we have established our origin and homage, let's look at the nature and power thereof;

"All flesh is not the same flesh: but there is one kind of flesh of men, another flesh of beasts, another flesh of fishes, and another of birds. There are also celestial bodies, and bodies terrestrial: but the glory of the celestial is one, and the glory of the terrestrial is another. There is one glory of the sun, and another glory of the moon, and another glory of the stars: for one star differeth from another star in glory. So also is the resurrection of the dead it is sown in corruption: it is raised in incorruption: It is sown in dishonour; it is raised in glory: it is sown in weakness; it is raised in power: It is sown a natural body, it is raised a spiritual body. And so it is written, The first Adam was made a living soul; the last Adam was made a quickening spirit." - 1 Corinthians 15:39-45 KJV

This describes the different compositions of matter and its architecture which God has created as we've touched a bit on particle physics, and how we (spirit beings) in particular are housed in flesh and can function terrestrially. There is much more knowledge and power to be understood from these verses; the power of the resurrection Spirit - the same Spirit that raised Jesus from the dead, the same Spirit that was promised to us that He will live in us. The scripture teaches us also the sow and reap principle God has established, however, we do get the basis of who we are and the working nature and power of our God the Creator.

God gave Adam authority and put him as a caretaker of all things created on earth. Adam unwittingly renounced his position by dishonoring God. Hence man started living under the curse of the law. The law was established to show man how erroneous he was living. Man died towards God, he became more carnal; earthier, sense ruled. Satan took authority (Adamic authority) as a result and became ruler of this world. How did Jesus Christ restore all that was stolen? He knew His mandate; He knew His purpose for being born a human being like you and me. His birth was revealed long before He was born, and Satan sought to eliminate Him in many ways through kings and rulers. The devil knew Jesus was the Son of God to save mankind but didn't know how God was going to do it. Hence, He tempted Jesus on many occasions. Jesus didn't fight evil with physical weapons - it wasn't going to get the job done. His life was as God intended man to live: faith through right standing with God. Then He could do anything through God in Him. The Adamic authority Satan had, had to be dethroned through truth, which the devil attained through deception creating the sinful nature of humans. Jesus became sin itself on the cross to displace its power, hence He said it is finished when He died. He had proved His obedience to the will of God even unto death. The battle was won in the spirit. He couldn't be tempted by evil, He couldn't succumb to human beings' opinions of Himself, and neither did He fear death. He died and faced the devil and his cronies in the pit of hell and He took back all power and authority over all things, and the keys to life and death because He had nothing in common with evil.

"For we wrestle not against flesh and blood, but against principalities, against powers, against the rulers of the darkness of this world, against spiritual wickedness in high places." - Ephesians 6:12 KJV

"For though we walk in the flesh, we do not war after the flesh: (For the weapons of our warfare are not carnal, but mighty through God to the pulling down of strong holds;) Casting down imaginations, and every high thing that exalteth itself against the knowledge of God, and bringing into captivity every thought to the obedience of Christ; And having in a readiness to revenge all disobedience, when your obedience is fulfilled." - 2 Corinthians 10:3-5 KJV

Hence, He said to forgive them for they know not what they are doing. Spiritual intelligence is key, without it, life becomes a mystery. The reason the above scripture says we should not or do not fight human beings of flesh and blood is that it is pointless, why? if you lose in this world it is because you have already lost first in the spirit realm. The battle lost there, manifests itself in the natural. Every country, every city, and every neighborhood has wicked rulers of darkness; territorial demonic spirits responsible for the administration of all these geographical areas using influence and covenants with people. Some people will outright sell their souls for money, power, or fame. We are in an era where false ministers are in contracts with marine spirits to capture audiences to fill their churches to gain popularity and wealth. Jesus warned us about them, and He said you will see them by their fruits - results. Thank God for scripture, as it is easy to pinpoint ministries with demonic influence. Their teachings are not consistent with the scriptures, it is just sad that their congregants do not study the word for themselves. It is important to first seek the kingdom of God, and not money or material things. The lesser is included in the greater, money is just a derivative in the kingdom. And don't be fooled and buy into the norm that preachers or Christians aren't supposed to be rich or wealthy, this is not a sign of false prophets or a church. It is emphatic that all true Christians are, or ought to be wealthy.

Proverbs 22:4 says, "The reward of humility and the reverent and worshipful fear of the Lord is riches and honor and life".
"And I will give you the treasures of darkness and hidden riches of secret places, that you may know that it is I, the Lord, the God of Israel, Who calls you by your name" – Isaiah 45:3.
"The blessing of ADONAI is what makes people rich, and He doesn't mix sorrow with it." – Mishlei (Proverbs) 10:22 CJB.

And there are replete passages about Christians and wealth. Ministers of the word are supposed to be ballers unless it is your choice not to participate in the Commonwealth. The fruits of falsehood are generally unsettling and unethical practices, even if you are patient, you always have doubt and never come to peace or satisfactory conclusive answers to your questions. Remember, preachers are people, they are susceptible to everyman's shortfall, but their cases are not extreme and they fix their mistakes. God's ministers' prosecutions do not last and most of the time are proven to be false accusations, and no matter what governments try to do regarding their wealth, they cannot touch them because that is a blessing from God and not of this world system. But the false preachers' cases and judgments will always appear plain as day. However, as a note of caution, it is not our place to speak against any minister, it is against God's will. Never utter a word against them, no matter how true, you do not know the story and you don't want to be part of it. Just sit back and watch, it will be evident. These are the strongholds we fight against, but you cannot defeat them with physical weapons. In Daniel 10, an angel came to Daniel while he was fasting to let him know that he was delayed due to his captivity by the spirit Prince of Persia (demonic ruler over the then kingdom of Persia, which was under king Cyrus on the earth) to deliver his message, but he was rescued by Michael the Archangel (angel then guarding over Israel). The angel also warned Daniel that the Persian Prince will be joined by the counterpart Prince of Greece to make war against God's angels. How strong are your angels, do they have to be rescued as well?

As I discussed earlier on how the enemy capitalizes on getting people as emotional as possible to cloud their judgment, he wants to influence you to manipulate the one thing humans have that no other in creation possesses: the ability to imagine. Imagination is the number one tool to create, which is what the devil is after to power through our lives. He doesn't have it, so he will try to create things for the future using your imagination, by using any possible way to get thoughts to your mind so you can imagine that which is contained within those thoughts. As you continually and unconsciously think, imagine, and speak, you create an unwanted carefully planned outcome. Why? Because many are led not to believe in daydreaming. So they do it unawares, manufacturing things they'd rather not have.

You may ask, how can I control my thoughts? Let's first answer why you aren't able to control them. This is because of how we grow up being dictated to by our environment and indoctrinated by the world's systems and knowledge. It is the negative words spoken to you, and the fear that has sponsored every action we take. Then this has become a way and pattern of thinking. There is a custom program that you have adopted over the years and it needs to be rewritten.

The passage above also says when your obedience is fulfilled, meaning when you have soaked yourself in God's word which is your weapon; you will have the readiness to speak against and pull down the strongholds (wrong mindsets, wrong beliefs, wrong thinking, demonic influence, and powers, etc) you face, which acclaim to be rulers or above God's creation - You, by bringing them into captivity. When you have come to a resolution for a better life, you will learn how to wield the spoken word against oppression in its entirety. You overcome unfavorable thoughts by addressing them directly with words. For instance, if you constantly think you are going to die, you ought to say; "I bind and hold that thought into captivity, I release the supernatural power of the Spirit of God to forget. I will not die, but I will live, with long life, I am satisfied, and no weapon formed against me shall prosper, for He that is in me is greater than he that is in the world. Jesus came that I may have life, and have it to the fullest till it overflows". You are affirming your knowledge and position, you know who you are and what you want. You are consciously functioning under grace and responding by using your sword which is the word of God, choosing to forget and to ponder on this old way of thinking. If such a thought comes four times in a minute, then you respond accordingly. Sooner or later you will find yourself having to fight better battles in life than the old ones. So, it is sometimes hard to control incoming thoughts because these are often from the subconscious, which is what you have previously dwelled on. A favorable thing to do is to reprogram what you knew with the new truths. The old way will fall away, and you will find yourself pondering on good things and you will be amazed that this is truly possible.

The devil has been defeated, all he uses is pressure and fear, so you put more opposing pressure as well and he will flee, he is a very proud being. Take note that God's power cannot flow accordingly where there are doubts and fear, He did not give you the spirit of fear, but of a sound mind and love. He keeps on saying do not fear because He wants you to know that He is with you. He has good thoughts and plans for you, and to give you hope for the future. If you look for Him wholeheartedly, you will find Him. He says He will end your captivity, bring you home and restore your fortunes.

We need to understand the war at hand, who we are, and what we are equipped for battle with. Only when we comprehend these mechanics and where we stand, we are consequently changed for the better through the knowledge of God imparted to our spirits.

These are the unseen forces and activities superimposing to affect the physical world.

When you sit and think about this, you start realizing that this world, realm, or dimension of the invisible things; imagination, words, particles – whether waves or energy, thoughts, and so on, all pre-exists and are required to create matter in the natural world at any given moment.

The supernatural does exist, and as it is self-explanatory, super in the supernatural is superior to the natural, the physical nature of existence.

CHAPTER 6
Reasons To Despise Illicit Drugs

We all have the innate ability to fight for success and to pursue to thrive. The paths we choose to take can determine our destinations, and the type of path can indicate a probable destination. The type of characters you choose to be with on that path can influence your life experience and where the journey might take you. Those characters you chose can indicate the type of activities to expect, and they will surely attract opportune events creating a fitting end. But there are unpredictable hurdles on every path. And these hurdles have origins and purposes, either to test or to harm. This will tell you who put the hurdle there. It will either make you stronger should you have the right training or it will destroy you if not helped.

Every person knows when he or she is doing or planning anything inappropriate, unlawful, dishonest, illicit, or crooked, as an instigator, or being influenced. It is the habit of doing this that gives one the courage to keep at it and disregard ethics. One might say that they are indifferent about the matter or couldn't care less (which is superficial), but the forces, authorities, and principalities of this world care about how you are influenced and how you influence others. And their concern isn't about your emotions and well-being, but how you live in society.

You are not a factor to evil forces once you are sloppy and irresponsible about your life, because it's easier for you to be influenced to be a party to destruction. And ultimately this doesn't earn you accolades, but disregard and suffering. Adverse conditions will make any person acknowledge that they care deeply about themselves irrespective of what they thought they knew yesterday. But it is God that immensely cares for you, even your family and friends most often.

I don't want the above to be lost in translation. So let me explain. There's looking after oneself; hygiene, health, security, and so forth. There are self-concerns; what you will eat, how you will get there, when will this or that be, who loves or hates you. Then there's self-love; emotional well-being, self-prioritization, self-improvement, being cautious of environmental influences, etc. We could consider someone to be well-rounded when they look after themselves, are sober-minded to think about the future, and love themselves. We can safely translate this concept that the person "cares" about their life. However, it is often difficult especially for teenagers to comprehend that trouble is around the corner when they hang around bad company, which most of the time are the cool guys. Tell someone who just started using drugs to stop because it's going to ruin their future then you'd sound like a false prophet. They won't believe you. You would become an enemy of progress to them.

Food turns out to be an overrated commodity to a druggie. Savings becomes a thing of the past, cash is king and it's needed now. Daytime is sleeping time because freaks only come out at night. Clubbing every day is now a norm followed by secret locations where the tongue gets loose with words that sink ships. Then new circles, new vibes, and new places make you forget everything current and old – you are always high as a kite. You start becoming a mystery to those who know you; at home, at work, and to old friends. Relationships collapse because of lies and inconsistencies. Finances and favors then dry up. You'd be lucky to save a job. You then blame people for not helping, which is passing responsibility, and this is handing over your power. Your outlook on life becomes resentful because of how things are turning out. At this point, self-love doesn't feature anywhere in your consciousness. You can't look after yourself, half the time you find yourself waking up in unfamiliar places with no toiletries and clean clothes. This makes you wear strangers' clothes as you hardly go home, and your identity gets buried in all this. Now, if you don't have an income, your new buddies can't give you a fix for free all the time, you must be resourceful.

As a youngster, theft starts at home, and as an adult, you will start dealing in illegal means all just for a fix. Soon you are indebted to drug dealers then the fun begins. This position will now make you disregard caution because you have to do anything in your power to pay the debt even to get more drugs. Your safety and other people's well-being aren't a concern to you anymore. It wouldn't matter anymore whether you defraud, steal or kill. Does this sound familiar? The enemy comes only to steal and kill. Care goes out the window.

To realize that odds are against you indicates you have gone wrong somewhere. It is important to notice that a realization just doesn't come, but it's influenced by some sort of drive from within, emerging from a difficulty, or motivation from passion to attain change or results. This is so because you have chosen to look at your position and weigh in to resolve your survival. This comes from you being conscious of influences surrounding you, and the choices to opt for. It proves that you are intelligent enough to reconcile your life and capacitate your mental aptitude for a better outcome. The flip side of being optimistic and proactive is being pessimistic and passive. You see what is going on but you chose to put the blame elsewhere and not to dig deep to understand the situation, rather you sit back and hope for a miracle.

Miracles do happen, and they are part of the Christian life, however, they just don't happen from thin air, you work out your own miracles, that is; you take from the knowledge what the word of God says about your situation, then you apply that principle in faith, then God responds to you according to your faith. The worst is when you are in a position where you have led yourself to be swallowed up by earthly elements, where life gets so desperate and grave that anything goes. This shouldn't be.

Life's journey has many hurdles hence it is best to ask when unsure about some things so that we can prepare and equip ourselves ahead as much as possible to enhance the probability of a winning chance when the need comes. And this is purely from the natural standpoint of any normal dependency-free individual. With drug-associated influence, you reduce your success likelihoods, you get into a battle with your hands tied, and you are no Bruce Lee in life's higher matters. We all desire to be champions, but nothing worth having comes easy, and such demands hard work. This calls for acknowledging and respecting the power in processes. Taking the initiative and the first step will kill procrastination, taking you out of your comfort zone and being determined to face challenges head-on with a never-die mentality.

Some people who choose to engage in criminal activities usually have an above-average intellect or talent of some sort but fail to channel this in the right direction, they instead opt for quick fixes. Reasons being redemption from poverty, but get into these dealings with no sustainable objective plan, then get swallowed by greed, and pride buries them.

It is fairly easy to fall victim to your craftiness in dishonest trades. Creation is balanced and self-sustained by its principles, we only fit in to manifest the framework of the perfect picture from that which we have chosen: that which you choose to be or give out returns usually multiplied, pleasing or unpleasant. In whatever you do, never overestimate yourself to be above these universal principles. Yet through egotism, some tend to mock the Grand Master of these laws.

It had been years later after I had chosen to be on the straight and narrow, leaving the life of crime behind, when I returned home to find that my wife and two kids had been held under house arrest by criminals and our belongings were stolen. By the grace of God, they were not harmed. Things have been stolen from me before, it was no issue, and this time I was also not concerned about what was taken. And yes, even when I was a thief I did think about karma, we all do at certain moments, however, my rationale was that I am a thief, I never confront anyone to put their life in jeopardy, they are only surprised when they found out. So was I also regrettably astonished when I found this happening at my home. With reflection I realized that I had never been so afraid in my life, it might be because material things never meant much to me, but those I so dearly love being in that predicament made me grasp how easily we misconstrue and undermine what would or would not hurt the next person because of our actions. I had never imagined my family being in that position, yet it hit home the least I expected. I was like a raging bull, but there was nothing I could do, rather count my blessings and appreciate my family even more.

Life always gives back the taste of that medicine you always dispense. If it's good deeds you do, keep at it, and if not, the sooner you retract your steps and repent the better because there is always grace especially when you heed that soft voice inside you to make changes. I'm addressing this to the drug dealers and the gangsters.

You might think you are cold to this, but it is exactly that, emotions from the thoughts you have put at the forefront of your brain because of all the nasty things life has given you, but that is no excuse, it is you that have led yourself here, there is a knowing on the inside of you. You might be a block of ice, yet this ice has a constant burning on the inside. I would say thug to thug, but I'm not a thug anymore. Putting up with a gangster demeanor just to portray your confidence and dominance is tiring, always on guard and you know that this is not the best of you. Most often, thugs are the most loving and caring people I'd ever known, but contrary to this, you think you wouldn't give a hoot about a stranger, which is a lie, because, given an opportunity to meet and understand the next person, you fall in love easily and would do anything in your power to protect them. Yet again, when you mature, the things you do bothers you, constantly so. For new change to come, the current system must collapse first, and you know it.

For every fish, there's a bigger fish, and for every bigger fish there's a smaller parasite sent forth to destroy, then there's the Observer! The biggest and scariest gang banger is often shot down by the young monkey-turned-gorilla.

There's an aspect of fear and death I have come to understand and here it is;

Fear of the unknown. A seasoned and highly reprehensive felon seldom thinks back to how it was the first time they committed an offense. It took much courage, there was a fear factor from panic, and their spirit cautioned them not to proceed, but had to go ahead because of a push from a certain influence. This type of fear is the corrupt version of God's given courage. Let me explain; God said to Joshua *"do not fear but have courage"*. And again, the fear of the Lord doesn't translate as "to be afraid of God" but "to have reverence for God". The devil knows how to and *is* the corruptor of truth and correct language. Courage can be displaced into fear. This character now lacks the courage for a clear-headed approach to appropriate situations and courses of action but is driven by fearful decision-making of retribution. It is easy to lie to get out of a tight corner because you are afraid of punishment, contrary to having the courage to own up to bad actions and turn a new leaf. This cover-up repeats to keep one in a perpetual state of fear-driven decisions and actions for self-preservation.

A child might hide the truth by being afraid of punishment from parents, a criminal afraid of jail time, and a hitman afraid of a cartel boss but not prison. The reasons are endless, but the ultimate thought is being afraid to die. Let's look at the heights of this territory and its status quo. Some people think death leads to nothingness, to seize to exist, yet are afraid when the opportunity presents itself due to uncertainty, and also the love of life, its pleasures, and aspirations. The hardcore and stone-hearted find death not intimidating because of this nothingness. But it is the pain and suffering they've experienced themselves, and that which they've inflicted on others, and a sense of giving up - whatever will be let it be! This is a lack of understanding the gravity of the situation. Gangsters get taken over by a force, and by the way, no gangster refers to themselves as a gangster when in the game, this is a societal description to them. Sometimes death is no threat in this case because of the state of mind. Hence some are feared more than others and taking someone's life is not much of a thing. This is a spiritual domain where such a person operates from, even if they don't know it and think death leads to nothingness or, whatever will be will be. Such was Jimmy, and a gentle giant he was, yet nothing could get in his way when he had an assault rifle in his hands, and his mind was set on that armored vehicle. It's like having two different personalities. Schizophrenic if I might add. He met the very same fate, multiple gunshot wounds from an AK. I couldn't contain myself when I got the call of his death, I cried so much I had to pull my car over. My tears can never change the course of eternity, however.

Let me come back to the context my brothers and sisters - the hardcore ninjas. You could be a runner, an enforcer, or the boss, we all must account. Not fearing prison or death is good, you were not meant to anyway, but not because of nothingness. The truth is more chilling and that is what you must be wary of: being outside of God.

"There was a certain rich man, which was clothed in purple and fine linen, and fared sumptuously every day: And there was a certain beggar named Lazarus, which was laid at his gate, full of sores, And desiring to be fed with the crumbs which fell from the rich man's table: moreover the dogs came and licked his sores. And it came to pass, that the beggar died, and was carried by the angels into Abraham's bosom: the rich man also died, and was buried; And in hell he lift up his eyes, being in torments, and seeth Abraham afar off, and Lazarus in his bosom. And he cried and said, Father Abraham, have mercy on me, and send Lazarus, that he may dip the tip of his finger in water, and cool my tongue; for I am tormented in this flame. But Abraham said, Son,

remember that thou in thy lifetime receivedst thy good things, and likewise Lazarus evil things: but now he is comforted, and thou art tormented. And beside all this, between us and you there is a great gulf fixed: so that they which would pass from hence to you cannot; neither can they pass to us, that would come from thence. Then he said, I pray thee therefore, father, that thou wouldest send him to my father's house: For I have five brethren; that he may testify unto them, lest they also come into this place of torment. Abraham saith unto him, They have Moses and the prophets; let them hear them. And he said, Nay, father Abraham: but if one went unto them from the dead, they will repent. And he said unto him, If they hear not Moses and the prophets, neither will they be persuaded, though one rose from the dead." Jesus told this story in Luke 16:19-31

Hell was not created for human spirits, but for demons and fallen angels.

Some people do rituals to get what they want, and unknowingly open unsavory doors to oppression and we later think it is just a mental or a medical condition. The devil doesn't like you and he won't even after death. He hates people and has no mercy whatsoever. When you are in his territory, he doesn't play nice.

There are many playgrounds, yet these are dangerous grounds. Grounds counterfeited against the earnest creation and inevitably to be ruined. Which fish are you? I don't want to engage too much in this, but this is a deception game. The bully Megalodons at the top who owns major corporate firms – the Corporatocracy influencing the bank's monetary systems are the ones controlling the global influx of drugs, using their economic hitmen through government agencies to fund their complex systems implemented in the very same government offices as regulatory policies, and utilizing and rendering specific military agencies immune to oppress the very same Cartels they get the product from let alone the rest of the population – the deep state. It has always been and will always be a setup; you go down screaming and kicking, dropping names, but you can't touch them, they are protected by their own rules.

53

"Can a blind man guide and direct a blind man? Will they not both stumble into a ditch or a hole in the ground" - Luke 6:39 AMP.

To them, it is no longer about possessions, which you seek, but arbitrating whether you, your family, or your race is worthy of what's considered an equal human being to their stature and a slave to their systems – a pawn. They consider themselves above you, and your fate should be decided for you. Both major and minor league dealers will always fall into this trap, there is nothing like not getting high from your own supply. The supply is within your reach, and there's a constant supply of problems with this trade. The higher you are in the pyramid, the more problems, the more you don't care, the higher you get from your supply, the harder you fall inevitably. Some also thought they could buy seats in parliament, buy law enforcement, sponsor politicians, etc. I don't want to mention names, but history shows us this principle in action. Only the elite influential shadowy megalodon sharks will remain for a while though. Yes you are already in their system, you want money and would do anything for it - but there's a higher wealth system already in place before this was fabricated; the supernatural law of provision and multiplication:

"Judge not, and ye shall not be judged: condemn not, and ye shall not be condemned: forgive, and ye shall be forgiven: Give, and it shall be given unto you; good measure, pressed down, and shaken together, and running over, shall men give into your bosom. For with the same measure that ye mete withal it shall be measured to you again." - Luke 6:37-38 KJV

Swim in a different stream while time allows. Learn to trade in a new industry and change with time. Don't find yourself in the future being helpless, monopolized with no options but to be someone else's slave, feeling sorry for yourself or those you love. And that time is nearer than you think. The rest are obvious issues in the destruction chain, killing each other over turfs and money, and setups to move more compromising the other. Incarceration has gone up over the years, especially for peddlers, many are given death sentences because the world is tired of kids dying from drug-related incidents.

The system's architecture is to have mules deliver a virus and infect as many people as possible, the infected members of society will directly or indirectly affect the larger global neighborhood, causing financial and biological dysfunction of the major society, taking back the money quickly to the corporations, leaving several people vulnerable and seeking aid in many areas of their lives. The caring must now invest time and money in helping, many families have to refinance from the same corporations to take their children to rehabilitation centres. This is but one device out of many.

You may have overlooked the severity of selling drugs; the retribution from the chain of command, and the lives you negatively impact by feeding their addiction. Sit and watch turf wars long enough, people killing each other mercilessly, and you will surely acknowledge that a person cannot hate another that much. It is the thing inside that person that drives them to kill. You can see it in their eyes. That thing is what hates human beings. You were not born to kill or be a vessel for a hateful demon.

To the end-user;

Here's my argument, before drug abuse you still had challenges to overcome. Financial freedom is at the top, or maybe being in good health. Every family unit requires a continuous supply of money to sustain a good livelihood if not a great one. However, your brainpower is the key that has to come up and sustain this financial planning. You were still figuring out how to be successful before you took drugs, but then, what happens when you mess with the one resource you have as an advantage – your mind?

Some have done great with their lives and then got into drugs. I know young medical doctors who take cocaine the whole night with no sleep, go home in the morning for a quick shower, get to their practice for a few consultations then knock off early for another line of coke. What happens then when you lose your license? It takes painstaking nine years of study to become a medical doctor, you've done it, and it was with a passion you did it, and this goes for all professions. Are you going to waste your life and dreams away for a night out with fake friends who are after your money? Half the time you can't even get it up anyway because you forgot to buy the blue pill. You then have to keep the bags coming just to hang around to score in the morning. If not retiring to porn to help yourself out. Come on, you are better than that. Life can't go on like this.

And we all know what happens when budgets are low, and you can't sustain the chase. There'll always be that guy who will suggest the next best drug. You move from back to worse – coke to rock and being a rock-star isn't cool at all – hell will be raised! I knew a friend of a friend who was doing well in construction, he had a beautiful house in a well sort-after estate, the latest model cars, and had a good personality – an insightful guy. Just to illustrate the earlier, his life went from back to worse. He did coke, his house was always occupied by friends. The weekends were worse, always a party. Dealers gave him consignments taking advantage of the clientele he had. Little did he know that he would get high from that supply and not sell it. I remember on some early hour mornings he would be broke, coming down and upset with those people in his house wanting freebies. He would give them corn power mixed with baking powder, and sadly they wouldn't even notice. Because with coke really, all it takes is the first few lines then the rest you are just chasing the high and many fail to recognize this.

There was this married lady he was dating. Let's name the above friend of a friend Jack. The lady's husband knew about the cheating and drug abuse. He had contacted Jack on numerous occasions warning him to stop the affair and giving drugs to his wife. He pleaded with Jack to stop allowing the wife to come to his house. They had two kids and he was not always home because he was a pilot and the kids were suffering due to the wife's addiction. The guy loved his wife, he put his pride aside and kept on urging Jack to stop the relationship. Jack would try keeping her at bay, but the lady persisted, and Jack would give in. Then came one night when the pilot stormed into Jack's house, straight up to the bedroom, and found his wife with Jack. Jack didn't hear his phone ringing when the security guards were trying to tip him that there was a guy with a gun coming. They tried refusing him access but he pulled out a gun and drove through the boom gate. The pilot shot his wife dead, shot Jack, and turned the gun on himself, leaving two kids with no parents.

Jack survived after a couple of weeks in the intensive care unit. I later found out that his parents had cut him off because he didn't stop with the drugs even after such an ordeal. He had turned to rock, crack cocaine. He later died of a drug overdose. This is but one story of many sad ones.

Another lost soul was a friend with great potential, an ex-Olympic medalist, and a great father he was. He had tried to commit suicide a couple of times after heavy nights of binging on drugs due to marital issues and the pressures of life. And yep, he finally did kill himself.

The other with whom I don't want to get into details is also another friend. What I would only like to highlight is when I talk about the power of speech, especially when you mean it. As I earlier said, users tend to praise drugs or the experience. Now, this friend was one cool cat, even before substance abuse. He was a focused chap, taking care of the family business, and his career here and there, and all his friends loved him dearly. Every time we'd hit, he would say "Now this is the sh*#* my friend, I'm gonna ride till I die" – meaning he's going to hit till he dies. Like many who love Tupac Shakur, so did he, and started voicing and correlating the lyrics from "Ambitionz Az A Ridah" because of how he perceived life to be with coke. But sadly he did ride till he died; he took his own life with a 357 magnum.

Success and fashion are to enhance one's appearance, especially in public, but moreover, it sure feels good after you've taken a good relaxing bath, and you get into the new clothes that fit you well and make you look even more outstanding. You sure feel like a million bucks. You can feel that spring in your step when you walk. But no matter what latest designer items you might have on, if you have that undesirable stench, math teeth, and skin from drug-related abuse, people are never really pleased to be around you, let alone your aura. And this is so saddening. Because at that stage all that matters to you is the approval of others. And these people are often the ones that are good for you, but such a reaction from them will have you return to the wrong crowd, those you take drugs with because your assumed thought is they will be happy with you and make you feel at home. And this is the trap, a vicious circle.

You can readily identify foul spirits with their foul smell, and as an addict, you carry this smell with you and are unaware of it, let alone the deterioration of your inner organs, facial skin, and teeth.

They say cocaine is a rich man's drug. Rationalizing this in monetary terms might be correct because it is an expensive habit, but I've seen rich people get broke from this habit. It doesn't just take what money you have or making but also alters how you operate, the ways and processes you made your initial growth with will be modified as a result of an addictive habit, leading to quick fixes which are not sustainable. So, drugs have no borders, doesn't matter what illicit drugs they are, cheap or expensive, the results are the same. This is not a habit you can keep up with economically. Unfortunately, some elites tend to think they are above the system.

Drug abuse leads to numerous health risks including unprotected sex leading to HIV and AIDS. Men are generally weaker than women when it comes to sex and control. In these circles, a promiscuous woman who is wrapped in this cloud is quite dominant and a high-risk factor, and should a guy find himself with a beautiful lady who wouldn't care about or prefer not to use a condom, the guy would fall and find himself having sex with no protection, which is what most prefer. And so the same is a woman who takes drugs depending on a guy who is reckless and wants things his way or no drugs. Let alone other inconceivable sexual acts induced by drugs, like orgies.

Drug paddling is a filthy trade. Lots of people lose their lives in the process. The war between Cartels themselves kill hundreds of thousands of innocents. And as an addict, you are sponsoring this trade to massive losses of human lives. There's tons of information on the internet with statistics should you wish to find out more about drugs, and programs like Drug Inc. should be informative.

Drug dealers don't have much respect if not at all for users. Why should you expose yourself to so much indignity to mules who wouldn't give a hoot about you? Why should you beg for your hard-earned belongings to be taken away for a hit? Why should you beg to be destroyed? Why should you waste your life away? Why should you hurt your family, the people who care about you the most, your mother, your father, your sister, your brother, and your children? Don't let drug dealers look at you and think you are a piece of you know what! At the same time, you are enriching the very same people who'll spit in your face with disgust! When you owe them, they supply a below-standard product than usual. Others are intentionally killed with drugs laced with poison because of debt.

Don't put yourself through the nonsense, you have a choice. Life or death is before you – choose life. It doesn't matter what background you come from, rich or poor, learned or not, you must retain your dignity. In my mother tongue, we say "Modidi o o makgakga!" meaning "A proud poor person!" You cannot afford to be trampled upon. You are fearfully and wonderfully made!

"Through skillful and godly Wisdom is a house (a life, a home, a family) built, and by understanding it is established [on a sound and good foundation], And by knowledge

shall its chambers [of every area] be filled with all precious and pleasant riches." - Proverbs 24:3-4 AMP
"Do you see a man diligent and skillful in his business? He will stand before kings; he will not stand before obscure men." - Proverbs 22:29 AMP

God will give you foresight into what you ought to become, choose and acknowledge that vision, He will give you insight into it, and He will also give you instructions on how to achieve that.

When you choose to operate with excellence and diligence in your life, you will surely find yourself in a position of authority and influence, not only for yourself but to help others as well. Isn't it odd that God shows us that there are insignificant people (obscure men, useless men, vain men, nobodies)? " *…men will have to give account for every idle (inoperative, nonworking) word they speak." - Matthew 12:36 AMP*. The value of your personality comes out of your mouth, your words locate you, and if your words are without value and are vain, you do not add value to yourself or anybody else. These are people who don't count; what they say doesn't matter, and what they do doesn't matter. And no one can make a nobody out of anybody, except themselves. Everybody has the opportunity and potential of being someone important in their lives and someone else's – man was made important first, but because of what comes out of their mouths, they have devalued themselves, and have to pay for it. Retract and repent (change your mind)!

Repentance simply means a change of heart and mind to turn away from sinful ways, motivated by love for God and a sincere desire to obey His commands. It's a choice to embrace God's love. When you consent, you allow Him access to your life [ref: *Luke 15 (Joy shall be in heaven over one sinner that repenteth, more than over ninety and nine just persons, which need no repentance.)* and notice in this parable it is the shepherd that does all the work, leaving the ninety-nine non lost sheep and going to look for the one lost sheep, finding it, finding you; all that the lost sheep does is consent to be carried, it doesn't run away from the shepherd because for some reason it knows that it is lost and can recognize its owner, and the shepherd carries it home rejoicing, wanting everybody to celebrate with Him about His found sheep - you]. Also, repentance in the Lord is continuous, because you are being perfected by God's word as you are taken from one level of glory to the next as the word renews your mind, as it reveals more knowledge and wisdom to your spirit. The only duty you have is to retain this knowledge and constantly remind yourself who you are. Allow glory to prevail in your life.

Wake up and kick devils out of your life!

Let me dwell a little on this important part which is your life. God said I put before you life and death. He didn't only give us options, but guidance as well. He said to choose life. Deuteronomy 30:15-20. An untrained personality generally squanders his or her abundance in times of plenty, then later struggles with much through lack of foresight: referring to the well-being of mind and health and maybe finances in this case. But after much self-abuse, you end up having now to realize the depravity of this situation, this life you live is in jeopardy. My point is the supernatural principle of provision like the one I alluded to earlier, dictates that one must have something to work with (to give) in the event of increment requisites. Like the widow whose sons were about to be taken for slaves by her dead husband's creditor, got her miraculous increase by having a jar of oil in her house to work with. She had something for Elisha the prophet to work with. - 2 Kings 4

Moses knew that it was humanly impossible to get the Israelites out of Egypt, but God asked him what he had in his hand, and he said a rod. Later we know the rod of Moses became the rod of God. - Exodus 4. The same account was when Jesus fed five thousand people with five loaves of bread and two small fish. - *John 6. (And after they had eaten and were full, Jesus said to gather up the fragments that remain, that nothing is lost, which were now twelve baskets full.)* This is tallying, it is diligence. How much could have been wasted if they upped and left? Sometimes God says take care first of the waste in your life and I will take care of that which you want. Isn't buying drugs or excessive alcohol a waste of your money?

Do not find yourself without the ability or a thing for God to bless for your increase and benefit. Here's the thing, when sin is fulfilled, death comes. Whatever bad habit you do consistently, will lead to your demise. And when you are consumed there is little to none you can do. Can't be, don't find yourself dry and out! There is always something you can do even if you have nothing to give, and that is the service you can be increased with.

"It is more blessed to give than to receive" - Acts 20:35 KJV

Do you know that beggars suffer because of this principle? It is not a wise thing to do, because the person who gives is the one that gets multiplied. Receiving is an endpoint if you don't give out a portion of that which you received – Saw and Reap. What you have is all you need to be increased with. You must always have a seed! It's better to have multiple seeds, for multiple harvests ☺ You plant intentionally with a plan and expect results, consciously so. I had to make up my mind and commit to using my talents to serve in the church and be a blessing to the ministry work. It takes a conscious decision to say I can do this and that. God will surely take that and multiply you.

It's your life and your responsibility. Be kind to yourself in every way possible. Your spiritual intelligence growth comes first!

Drugs equal activation of poverty and destituteness, then death – this is why you must loathe them. It is better to put gas in your car to go to work and earn than to make an excuse to be away from work.

"But seek ye first the kingdom of God, and His righteousness; and all these things shall be added unto you" - Matthew 6:33 KJV

What are you going to choose?

CHAPTER 7
How to Stop Using Drugs

"Beloved, I wish above all things that thou mayest prosper and be in health, even as thy soul prospereth." - 3 John 1:2 KJV

We have explored a variety of constructs with an intent to articulate the synergy of creation; how all things work together for an expected purpose or outcome. With this overview, we get to understand the world around us and how with a deliberate aim, one can affect and effect changes on things visible, or invisible by choosing not to be a victim but exercising power and authority over all else. Let's recap for a refresher on the subject of power and authority to rule over this fallen world.

The Adamic authority was stolen to rule over the earth, then came the corruption of humans, its knowledge, then the human DNA, producing Nephilims, who continued to ruin everything. These fallen angels know the rules of engagement. They influenced and then corrupted the human race and its estate, and due to a lack of awareness of principles governing events in this realm, man has been oppressed. As they say, the devil's biggest trick was that he doesn't exist. God even regretted creating human beings, but He had *the plan* to fix everything.

Jesus got baptized and received the Holy Spirit's indwelling. Then God said: *"This is My beloved Son, in whom I AM well pleased and delighted!"* – *Matthew 3:17 AMP.*

Later in Caesarea Philippi, in Bashan, on a rocky terrace of the foothills of Mount Hermon He said that He would build His church upon that rock and the gates of hell shall not prevail against it. He will give the church keys of the kingdom of heaven, and whatever we bind on earth will be bound in heaven, and whatever we permit on earth will be permitted in heaven. He then later took Peter, James, and John to the mountain where He was transfigured.

The three witnessed Jesus transforming into a divine being, and there appeared Moses and Elijah. The whole of creation witnessed ground zero, the very mountain where the fallen angels first set foot on earth; this was a public declaration to things in heaven, on the earth, and to the underworld. God then again said: *"This is My beloved Son, My Chosen One; listen and obey and yield to Him!"* – *Luke 9:35 AMP.*

"Therefore, God elevated him to the place of highest honor and gave him the name above all other names, that at the name of Jesus every knee should bow, in heaven and on earth and under the earth, and every tongue declare that Jesus Christ is Lord, to the glory of God the Father." – *Philippians 2:9-11 NLT*

God saw fit that the God-Head should be in Jesus, and as He resurrected He said: *"I have given to them the glory and honor which You have given Me, that they may be one, just as We are one;"* – *John 17:22.* This is our rightful position, the glory, and the honor is given to us, in our Lord Jesus Christ. We should work it from the inside out. It is a choice to be part of the scriptural prophecy. Remember as it happened when John thought he wasn't good enough to baptize Jesus? He said to John:

"Permit it to be so now, for thus it is fitting for us to fulfill all righteousness." – *Matthew 3:15.*

And again, in Luke 4 Jesus is handed the book of the prophet Isaiah to read from. He opened it, and it read:

"The Spirit of the LORD is upon Me, Because He has anointed Me to preach the gospel to the poor; He has sent Me to heal the brokenhearted, to proclaim liberty to the captives and recovery of sight to the blind, to set at liberty those who are oppressed; to proclaim the acceptable year of the LORD." – Luke 4:18-19

He didn't proceed but closed the book soon after the above, and told those who were there, "Today this Scripture is fulfilled in your hearing". Prophecy unfolded right before their eyes: His first coming was God's grace for us, He didn't proceed to read and mention *"And the day of vengeance of our God"*. This is spared for his second coming, which is very near. It will all be fulfilled.

Once upon a time just as it might be with you now, when life was difficult for me and I was looking for answers, I heard that all I needed was on the inside of me. But this was hard to believe nor come to terms with what it meant. This didn't make sense at all, and neither could I comprehend how the life I had would translate into the life I wished for. Was this literal or metaphoric I asked myself. Either way, there was no sense in what they said; All that you need is on the inside of you. No matter how happy I wanted to be, I just couldn't say or feel that I am happy and wishfully become happy with all the misery and misfortune I was facing. But have you realized how such sayings or things continue to show up every time you are looking for answers like something is toying around with you? How come the wealth of the world is in the hands of the few? Could it be that they are willing to do what others are not willing to do? Many say I want a change for the better, but how resolute are they about it?

Yes, it's all about being firm in your decisions, and your actions going forth will be evidence of what you are pursuing. The moment there is no friction with "All you need is on the inside of you", that will be proof positive that you are willing to learn and accept that you can't know what you don't know. Be humble enough to accept that there is more to life than you understand. Your willing heart will surely attract the knowledge you require for change. I said it made no sense, but that's exactly what my dilemma was; I was using my senses to want to grasp things unbeknown to me. My willingness to let go of what my environment had dictated and influenced me with, exposed me to knowledge and understanding leading to an inevitable change. I had made a choice, and there it was in front of me; seek first the kingdom of God, and all these things shall be added unto you. Yes, it was still raw and my mind still said this is far-fetched. And the scripture carries on saying; Fear not little flock for it is the Father's good pleasure to give you the kingdom.

Now when you get to live the last part of this passage, it's an aha moment because the journey has proved that the word of God is truth and it's alive; In Luke 17 Jesus said: *"The Kingdom of God cometh not with observation: neither shall they say, Lo here! Or, lo there! For, behold, the kingdom of God is within you"*. And there it is; All you need is on the inside of you! That's what it meant, lol! And it is bigger than I could ever imagine: because it is more than I could fathom, with the little I now know about this kingdom, it propels me forward, and it works, yet I know there is more. It's a process, but when you work this thing called faith from the inside out, it's marvelous and exciting when you see the results. Life stops becoming a mystery, and you get to know how to handle situations.

There are not only tools on the inside of you to mend and craft life, but a whole kingdom is behind you, rooting for you. Oh, how God loves you! Look for Him and He will reveal Himself to you. The first thing you have to do is get born again and get baptized, which we will discuss below, and renounce the devil.

As random life can be and throw us off here and there, we have to come to a realisation that structure is important for stuff to kind of work.

We have presented various passages and ideas throughout this material so far to familiarize ourselves with understanding the subject matter. Now we must structure this information so you can follow specific steps to see results in your life. And again, there is no hard and fast way with this, it is my experience that I am sharing, just let God work with you: He treats us differently with care when we yield to Him. While we are on this point, let's demystify how God sees you from what religion has taunted all these years. Can Jesus die for you and not accept you for drinking liquor, taking drugs, partying, or being so-called ungodly? Matthew 26:39 says Jesus fell on His face and prayed to say *"O my Father, if it be possible, let this cup pass from me"*. Why you might ask? When you meditate on His request you get to see that it was not only a task of dying for His Father's children. He knew what was going to happen to Him: the physical pain to endure, the piercing words of hatred and rejection. He was not immune like we are not immune to pain. Could we have done this for anyone? The worst, however, with no better vocabulary to describe it, is becoming sin. That is when He cried out saying why have You forsaken me? It makes you wonder. Alas, God turned His back on Him. For who and for what was this for? There the earth quaked, the day was darkened, and the curtain was ripped from top to bottom. A passage for mankind to freely come to God through Jesus was established with no conditions. Now, tell me, for what can God not forgive you for? It was all for you. Religiousness is death, being in right standing through Jesus Christ is life. Be free and commune with your Father. It is His will.

Operating at your highest faith indicates that you are content and devoid of fear. You do not live in the past, but you displace any negativity with the active truths stored in your heart and understanding, and your present-day is nothing but rejoicing in what God has already provided. You do not have to wait to be happy, but your joy is proof of things not seen. Your present-day reflects your future. This is attainable, God wouldn't say it if it wasn't true. Remember, refuse to be distracted, you know what puts you down therefore refuse to focus on it and it will dissolve. Give energy to what propels you to your future. It is a practice, make this a habit.

The information you have gathered thus far from your environment is stored in your mind, and it is the driving force to your success or failure, hence God wills and advises us to renew our minds so that we can prosper. The sum of all this data in you has shaped some form of fears and mishaps leading to emotions being in charge to the greater extent of your soul's operations. For example, your mind says I don't know how to get out of this trouble, I don't have this or that, my life is in ruins, blah blah blah, lies and more lies – this is what you are accustomed to focusing on. Emotions whirl up and fear surges as per habit, and your emotions trigger alarms to the mind; this is bad, we must feel good, and the mind knows best how to adjust the preferred mood: "a bag of coke would be good right?" Now, this rhetorical question is posed to the will and its power to act. But that which is shouting the loudest in your soul is the emotions accompanied by this spirit of fear and the body's usual desires. Guess which part of your soul gets the attention and the upper hand ultimately? It is the emotions, and that influence the willpower to act out the mind's decision. So, the biggest dilemma here is the information stored and habits acquired throughout all these years to affect the sequence of events in the workings of your soul for outcomes. It is not easy to correct the process, but one must start to finish.

A viable approach and process for your soul is for the mind to compute the optimum possible rationale for the best results. Then your willpower to exercise its potential energy to act out the recommended motivation for an outcome that serves you well, even if you feel fear, and lastly you can enjoy the emotions that come with the results. This approach, however, is not the ideal process for your soul though, because with both above illustrations really, your soul is determining the character of your spirit, you, which should not be. Your soul is meant to reflect who you are - your spirit. The ideal working of your whole part as self is for you as a spirit to be in charge and in control of your soul and body.

Accurate information, knowledge, wisdom, and power come from God through His word. His word feeds your spirit, and your spirit should feed your soul everything that is connected to God, your body will then comply to act in line. Hope and faith will then rise.

"Faith cometh by hearing, and hearing by the word of God" - Romans 10:17 KJV

"I have no greater joy than to hear that my children walk in truth" - 3 John 1:4 KJV

Jesus Christ said, "I am the way, the truth and the life" John 14:6 – so the above scripture means I walk in Christ (He is the Truth). He is the way: my time and space are in Him. God foreknew you and predestined your life to be conformed to the image of Christ and that you may be justified and glorified – becoming the Word. Romans 8:29-30

"But as many as received Him, to them gave He power to become the sons of God, even to them that believed on His Name: Which were born, not of blood, nor of the will of the flesh, nor of the will of man, but of God. And the Word was made flesh, and dwelt among us, (and we beheld His glory, the glory as of the only begotten of the Father,) full of grace and truth." - John 1:12-14 KJV

As you read and study, understand, and choose to believe the Word of God for yourself. Those strongholds (mindset, imagination, bad habits, wrong beliefs, misinformation, dark forces, and false precepts) will dissolve.

Let us expand.

The determining factors between social classes are information, application of that knowledge, and their habits; whether goals are set or not, and the efforts taken to achieve those objectives. Many just hope without any action or plan, and a few take initiatives and hope for the best. You must believe in yourself that you can achieve that which you desire. It all starts with believing. This requires you to examine your belief systems because most of the time these are the difference between attaining and falling short. And more often the pieces of evidence that reveal our belief systems are in our quality of thoughts and manner of speech. "If anybody can do it, I can do it" or "I'm not fit to do this, I can't do this, it's too good for me, my family is poor, I don't have money, or I'm not cut out for that kind of success." People always give valid reasons as to why they do not or cannot attain certain things they would like to have. It can be past experiences or instilled opinions of others in them. These are the things you ought to recognize and acknowledge for what they are: they either serve you or do not serve your purpose in life. So, renew your mind and your beliefs, and replace everything that works against you on the inside with what resonates with the future you want, and work towards a healthier lifestyle. When you have come to this resolution, be patient and kind to yourself. If you are far from believing in God, try Him. With the little I know about Him; I can assure your victory.

It is imperative to take a hundred percent responsibility for your life and actions and do away with any sort of excuses. Authority means power and ability in hand. Now when you make excuses or want to blame someone or something, you are robbing yourself through this act consequently handing over your authority to whatever you blame. Soon it becomes evident of the inabilities you have brought to yourself.

Take stock of your life, and your achievements since you were born, doesn't matter how insignificant you think they are; what led to those successes must be enlarged in your life. And look at your mishaps; how you sponsored those unfortunate moments, and do away with the same kind of habits and choices. You are here in this position because you allowed it to happen, and that includes all areas of your life. You had choices to make, and you chose that which led you to the now. But now is the time to choose again. Tomorrow will be influenced by today's choices. Do not be a people pleaser, if something doesn't suit your plans, your answer should be a resounding "No."

Setting goals is a must if you are to achieve anything in life, and goals should be well thought out. Get material around this subject of goal setting, and learn more to give yourself an advantage towards the achievements you desire. You must have a vision, then imagine that which you wish for, and it must be clear in your mind. Specificity is important because you are telling your mind either to wonder or to figure out how to get to a specific thing. It's not wise to simply state that you want any type of car without giving any thought should you wish for one, because you may end up with a car you dislike and ultimately add to the list of things you are unhappy about your life. Rather say you'd like to have a black specific brand and year model car, that's if you like black. Jot down your specific goal and the date you wish to achieve it. Timing is important, even if at first you don't attain it at the set time, it takes practice. Sooner, your timelines to achieve things will be as you have set them. This is a skill on its own through understanding project management. Have a notepad with you always for reminding yourself, and copies of its visual content where you can readily see your goals. Recognize and acknowledge the emotions that you will have when you have accomplished your desires and have these feelings stick to you in the now and forge these emotions every day till your dream comes alive. Don't say I will be happy if I get such and such a thing, be joyful now, happy people in the now attract the things they desire and other good things they didn't think of because they themselves are the source of joy.

Write down also a strategic plan on how you will be able to achieve this goal, don't shy away and say I don't know how, answers are always there within reach. Pen down what you can, and keep developing and changing the plan continuously. Change is good, it is a natural process. This also proves to you that you are putting effort though things seem slow or unclear. You will find that every initiative you take gets the ball rolling, and you should consciously pat yourself on the back for every little step you take; you do what you can, and God will do what you cannot do. And be patient. Remember, it doesn't matter what your goals are, just do you, seek approval from yourself, then approve yourself.

Make time every day to focus on the vision, your notes, and your emotions, morning, noon, and night. Sponsor these by speaking to them, and energize the dream with increasing daily focus with joy as if it has happened already. Charge your vision before you sleep and when you wake up in the morning so that when your focus is on your day-to-day business, the vision remains energized till you come back to re-energize it. It's the same principle as your mobile phone's battery. It must always be alive.

Then develop habits that will enhance the chances of your success. If I want to be rich, I must know rich people's habits, positive ones of cause. And if I want a healthy physique, who else to copy but athletes.

Know and Exercise Your Authority and Power – A deliberate Exercise
- Re-position yourself for victory
- Know and constantly remind yourself who you are
- Know about and get your arsenal in place
- Know how to use your weapons
- Know how to create and recreate

Quitting substance abuse is a process, like anything else to attain, it should be a goal, and it also depends on how deep in it you are. Acceptance of your state is key to your success. It will take a conscious willingness to say I've had my share of this experience and I want to be a better person than this. It must be a firm personal choice to want to move on and be great.

Other people are strong-willed to go cold turkey on drug abuse, but we are not all the same hence my writing to you who require help. Most users find themselves in a vicious circle, not knowing why they are not able to stop. The yearn to quit is good, but not enough to get you through. Users often find themselves stating to others that they want to quit, to the point where they stop saying it because it gets too boring to their peers. After all, you still hit anyway. This is a factor that influences change quite often - peer pressure. Just because you say you want to stop even though you still take drugs doesn't mean you are lying.

I used to say to a friend with who I took cocaine that drugs don't have anything on me I know I will stop. I had said this because I once stopped for a year then I had a relapse. But God revealed to me that it was too late on the latter. I had returned to using drugs again so now only He can help, and I will not be able to do it on my own. I even thought I had done it by my own will, which was false, hence the relapse. I was on autopilot and had been helped without knowing and no lesson was learned.

It was on many occasions that this was reiterated, and my strength to stop was shown to fall short. I then later said to my friend, only if you give this burden to God, to help you stop, you will have a knowing inside you that He will win the battle for you. But you see, this assumed me a hypocrite because we were hitting even more. What gave me the guts to keep saying this was the comfortable relationship we had, he kind of understood me and my belief. I didn't say this to the wrong crowd where I would feel utmost ridicule.

So, this means you need someone who's on the same page as you, who understands and can relate to what you are saying or wish for. I'm only saying this as my experience and because this happens a lot of times in such circles, but I came to understand that you can't trust someone in the same situation as you, there is much deceit and falsity in this cloud. If there isn't anyone, don't go looking for someone, tell it to yourself. Then you must cut ties with groupies, and move away from the drug scenes.

"Oh, the joys of those who do not follow the advice of the wicked, or stand around with sinners, or join in with mockers. But they delight in the law of the LORD, meditating on it day and night. They are like trees planted along the riverbank, bearing fruit each season. Their leaves never wither, and they prosper in all they do." - Psalms 1:1-3 NLT

The enemy finds anything that he can use against you to put *pressure*. So, moving away from other drug users will reduce any kind of pressure from your surroundings or environment for you to perform. Obviously, at this point, you haven't stopped, and don't put pressure on yourself. We don't want you to feel anxious. You need to see why you are taking drugs and we will find out that there is no reason at all, this means you must take them alone if you have to, and analyze everything if this hasn't dawned on you.

Most importantly, consciously refuse to watch pornographic material, especially if you are a couple. This is a whole topic on its own. I've seen couples who hit break up because of drugs and porn. The sexual desires drive you to even want to do more drugs and other unsavory things and it doesn't stop. Porn is a definite NO! Get rid of all your collections, and wipe out all your devices. And stop shnuffing in your home where you live particularly when there are small children. These fowl spirits affect them a lot, you'll see kids waking up very tired and depressed in the morning and very unhappy unlike they usually are. Be as uncomfortable as possible when you do drugs. If you are tempted to take a line in the house, rather go outside and take one or two lines, then pop a sleeping tablet to work against and prevent a long night binge on the substance.

When you find that you feel like going out to friends who hit and you have a problem with alcohol, pop a sleeping pill whiles you are drinking as well because if you get tipsy, you are going to want another line, and soon you'll be driving out at ungodly hours. When pressure comes and you feel like you can't handle it, another sleeping tablet will do the trick.

These sleeping tablets are not the solution and can also become a bad habit, you ought to proceed with caution and seek medical advice from a professional practitioner. People have different medical conditions and these tablets might adversely affect one if overdosed. They just help your physical body to escape the cravings that may lead to adverse behaviors. Consider this my disclaimer as well.

What works is prayer and the Word. Pray, read, and study the bible and watch or listen to the audio bible, sermons, and teachings as often as you can, high or not, even if you don't understand what is being said, just read and listen. If you can, sleep with the audio bible on, or a recorded sermon that you feel resonated with you. A point will come where you will have no reason to pick up a phone to call a dealer or a friend for a line. Your appetite for food will start rising, feed yourself and enjoy food, it's good for you.

Now the routine is as usual, the only difference is you are doing things alone. What you resist might persist, but not being afraid of it, and confidently disapproving of it, it will fade away. And remember this is not hiding, you are being personal to get to a resolution; to see if drugs serve you, given who, where, and what you wish to become.

See this habit for what it is if you haven't. Step aside, look into it, and see what experience it has brought you to, and be wholly free again. When you start having recurring dreams of you taking drugs, and you wake up with that disbelief that you just took a line, it's a sure sign of winning the battle.

Let's dig into the solution:

Get Born Again and Have a Personal Relationship with God

Some individuals misunderstand the nature of a relationship with God, believing that they can pray on their own and do not need to attend church to know God. This is misguided and not in line with His will for people. This belief reveals a person's knowledge or lack thereof, and the state of their spiritual intellect regarding who they are, God, and His ways. As a result, people continue to struggle and are subdued by circumstances. Just as organized as our institutions are, and able to take students and transform them into skilled professionals in various fields, why should we think God's plans for us are mundane?

God does not simply hover around waiting for our prayers to try and help us when He can, He wants to guide us through our struggles and reveal Himself and His ways to us. As exemplified in the story of the Israelites, He took them out of misery (Egypt) to take them into His rest (The promised land), and in between, He revealed Himself and His ways, and lessons were learned. It is not that Christians don't have challenges; but these challenges do come, however, it is when you are conscious of who you are, seeing and acknowledging the works of God in your life, and overcoming these obstacles: not dealing with the same problem endlessly, because of knowing what He says with regards to dealing with things. This includes knowing how He says you must relate to Him, how to pray, when to pray, when not to pray but speak His will (which is His word concerning certain things), the list is endless, and you can only know these by going and learning in church with fellow Christians who are well vested in the word. We will cover some of these later so that you can see results in your life and be aware of when it is brewing in you for success. So yes, He takes you "out" of misery, to take you "in" His rest and right hand – position of power and authority.

The crucial first step, whether drugs or not, everybody needs *a personal relationship with God*. You need to *accept Jesus as your Lord and Savior*. You need to *be saved*. Your spirit needs to be recreated; you need to be born again. And you require *asking God to send down the Holy Spirit to live in you*. With God, all is simple, *ask and receive*, and don't complicate things. You just need to know what He says, and everything is in His word; read and study the bible. Don't be religious with God, *He is your Father* and you will relate with Him just like that - as a Father. Religion is manmade and has taken us far from God and has taught and instilled *wrong doctrines* in many of God's people.

Let's clarify the above: A personal relationship with God

"And I will walk among you, and will be your God, and ye shall be my people." - *Leviticus 26:12 KJV*

God loves us so much that He came to reconcile us back to Himself and not only that but to also put us back in the original position of power and authority to be rulers of our world. Even the angels couldn't understand, asking God who is a man (why is a man so important to You, as weak, slow, and inadequate as You have created man to be) that You have to go and visit him? God wants to live with and walk with you.

76

"For it pleased the Father that in Him should all fullness dwell; And, having made peace through the blood of His cross, by Him to reconcile all things unto Himself; by Him, I say, whether they be things in earth, or things in heaven. And you, that were sometime alienated and enemies in your mind by wicked works, yet now hath He reconciled in the body of His flesh through death, to present you holy and unblameable and unreproveable in His sight:" - Colossians 1:19-22 KJV

And He also said:

"THEREFORE BE imitators of God [copy Him and follow His example], as well-beloved children [imitate their father]. And walk in love, [esteeming and delighting in one another] as Christ loved us and gave Himself up for us, a slain offering and sacrifice to God [for you, so that it became] a sweet fragrance. [Ezek. 20:41]" - Ephesians 5:1-2 AMP

You can also pick up what He is not saying in the above passage, that He had already said; that we are created in His image and likeness, so we have that power and authority as He has, hence we ought to imitate Him in all things, and that you are a god. Don't live like a prince or a princess who is oblivious to his Father's kingdom.

When you accept His Son Christ Jesus and His finished work, you are presented unblameable and unreprovable in the Father's sight. You are then hidden and covered in Christ. You are put in the right standing with God. When it was His time to return to the Father, at His resurrection, Jesus said "the glory that You have given Me, I have given them." And "them" is them that have accepted Him as Lord and Savior.

How to get saved.

"Because if you acknowledge and confess with your lips that Jesus is Lord and in your heart believe (adhere to, trust in, and rely on the truth) that God raised Him from the dead, you will be saved. For with the heart a person believes (adheres to, trust in, and relies on Christ) and so is justified (declared righteous, acceptable to God), and with the

mouth he confess (declares openly and speaks out freely his faith) and confirms [his] salvation. The Scripture says, No man who believes in Him [who adheres to, relies on, and trust in Him] will [ever] be put to shame or be disappointed. [No one] for there is no distinction between Jew and Greek. The same Lord is Lord over all [of us] and He generously bestows His riches upon all who call upon Him [in faith]. For everyone who calls upon the name of the Lord [invoking Him as Lord] will be saved." - Romans 10:9-13 AMP

So, to be saved, you pray the prayer of salvation **out loud confessing and accepting Jesus Christ** *as your Lord and Savior* as below:

"Dear God, I come to you as a sinner. I believe in my heart that Jesus Christ is the Son of God and that He died for my sins, and God raised Him from the dead victoriously. I pray to You, God of truth, that you cleanse me with the blood of Jesus Christ and blot my sins away. I acknowledge and confess with my mouth that Jesus Christ is Lord. I accept and receive Jesus Christ as Lord over my life. Thank you, Father God, for accepting me as your child and forgiving me of my sins. I declare that I am free from sin and the curse of the law. I am born again. I am a new creation in Christ Jesus. I receive the abundance of grace and the gift of righteousness. I am the righteousness of God. In the name of Jesus Christ, I declare that I am saved. Amen."

If you have prayed this prayer out loud, you are saved and a child of God you are. You only need to pray this once, you only receive Jesus Christ in your heart once and for all.

This mystery is the crux of the solution to our salvation and livelihood, not only to be liberated from drugs but from everything. The creation process is hidden as your treasure in the above for you to live by, as a god who creates his or her life's experience.

We know that when you are born again, your spirit is recreated, meaning it does not have a past, all you see with the naked eye is the same old person, but that is the physical, the body, the recreated spirit on the other hand which is the real you, is in the spirit, where all is created.

Let us clarify this creating process.

"For with the heart man believeth unto righteousness; and with the mouth confession is made unto salvation." - Romans 10:10 KJV

[the heart is your spirit – your spirit is part of God – your spirit is god – and God believes – righteousness is rightness, being right – God is always right, if He says darkness is light, darkness will become light – you are always right – if God commands light out of darkness, the Holy Spirit, the doer of God's work does the job – now when you open your mouth and command light in your life, you will get the job done because The Holy Spirit and you are one – this is salvation!]

The above is a divine principle set out to create or recreate for divine purposes.

First Level of Creation

"With the heart": before you can have anything settled in your heart, it must start as a thought. Meditation on this thought leads to imagination, and only human beings have this. Whatever the polarity of the thought, from agreeing within during the thought process, you settle it in your heart (spirit). And this is a process from the mind (soul). This is the first level of creation. When it has been reiterated and agreed upon, it is created. But here the senses cannot relate. Only all which are operating in this realm know what has been done.

"Believeth unto": this believing is directional, for an outcome, experience, or product to be realized, it all depends if there was a strong belief in the thought, that evolved and created a thing in the first level of creation; the spirit realm. If there is no believing (trusting), it doesn't matter what is sponsoring the thought - polarity; negative or positive, if you don't believe it, it will never happen.

"Righteousness": as I said in this context it is the divine; love sponsored creativity. Creation in the first level is driven by thoughts of love, and you are right in whatever you create. Unfortunately, many produce the wrong right (manifesting something that doesn't serve your preference). When your creation is sponsored by wrong thoughts and you believe and agree with them, you are right at the end of the day, because you are the master, you are the creator. And you should be happy about the results because it is your creation. No one to blame. You just didn't know how right you were. Are you a god or what?

Second Level of Creation:

"And with the mouth": your mouth is a tool to project creating words agreed from the heart (negative or positive), not only to eat and kiss ("man shall not live by bread alone, but by every word that proceeds from the mouth of God"), physical food is for the body, but you are not only your body.

"Confession is made": these are words to be uttered with the mouth, which are from the very same thoughts you have agreed within. Hence when you return God's word to Himself is considered the highest form of creation, which is the ultimate: " ...the word became flesh." Speaking is very crucial if you are going to get results. That is why they say a quiet Christian usually suffers from obtaining results. This is also where prophecy and prophesying come in. Every Christian ought to prophesy, it is a general misconception that only prophets prophesy, but the context is missed: The Prophet is in its office, however, every child of God including the Prophet ought to utter words that will shape or frame what they would like to see in their lives or lives of others, which is to prophesy (speaking forth that which is desired, individually or as a corporation). On the other hand, the

Prophet can be shown a vision, to tell a prophetic message about a future event, interpret a message or other tongues, or, to convey a concern from God about someone or something.

"And He said unto me, Son of man, can these bones live? And I answered, O Lord God, thou knowest (meaning only God knows, we always think the responsibility lies with God). *Again He said unto me, Prophesy upon these bones* (God meant to speak to these bones, the bones were right in front of him, this is not true about future events), *and say unto them, O ye dry bones, hear the word of the Lord. Thus saith the Lord God unto these bones; Behold, I will cause breath to enter into you, and ye shall live: And I will lay sinews upon you, and will bring up flesh upon you, and cover you with skin, and put breath in you, and ye shall live; and ye shall know that I am the Lord. So I prophesied as I was commanded: and as I prophesied, there was a noise, and behold a shaking, and the bones came together, bone to his bone. And when I beheld, lo, the sinews and the flesh came up upon them, and the skin covered them above: but there was no breath in them. Then He said unto me, Prophesy unto the wind, prophesy, son of man, and say to the wind, Thus saith the Lord God; Come from the four winds, O breath, and breath upon these slain, that they may live. So I prophesied as He commanded me, and the breath came into them, and they lived, and stood up upon their feet, an exceeding great army.*
Then He said unto me, Son of man, these bones are the whole house of Israel (you)*: behold, they say, Our bones are dried, and our hope is lost: we are cut off for our parts. Therefore prophesy and say unto them, Thus saith the Lord God; Behold, O my people, I will open your graves, and cause you to come up out of your graves* (misery), *and bring you into the land of Israel* (your promised land, your future). *And ye shall know that I am the Lord, when I have opened your graves, O my people, and brought you up out of your graves, And shall put My Spirit in you, and ye shall live, and I shall place you in your own land: then shall you know that I the Lord have spoken it, and performed it, saith the Lord"* - Ezekiel 37:3-14 KJV

Third Level of Creation:

"Unto salvation": this is the manifestation stage of what you've created; by confessing and doing that which you can, professing constantly and giving thanks in advance for what you have received, being blessed with. Aligning your thoughts, imagination, words, and projected feelings of outcomes of the creation, vision, and imagery of what you want to be like or experience, and bring everything including those feelings to the now, owning it in the present. Correcting every negative thought or word or feeling contrary to be obedient to what you have confessed to being, and it will be.

This is the Three-Part you are at work with on a day to day, and hence operations are in three parts. It requires mastery because we are spiritual beings with souls in a physical body choosing experiences to re-member (Body of Christ) who we are by operating in a physical world. This is the reason some talk about the law of attraction sighting some power out there or the universe except for acknowledging God. The truth is replete in scripture. Knowledge has come and gone, lost through the ages, but why have the scriptures not been lost to time?

The Lord Jesus said heaven and earth will pass away, but His words will by no means pass away. Ref: Matthew 24:35.

"For as the rain comes down, and the snow from heaven, and do not return there, but water the earth, and make it bring forth and bud, that it may give seed to the sower and bread to the eater, So shall My word be that goes forth from My mouth; It shall not return to Me void, but it shall accomplish what I please, and it shall prosper in the thing for which I sent it" – Isaiah 55:10-11

Believe, and it will be as you have imagined and have said, it's only a matter of patience, which God tells it's a virtue. He created the plants in Genesis 1, but Genesis 2 explains that the plant hadn't grown because God hadn't made it to rain.

The Holy Ghost

Now, the next step is to receive the Holy Spirit to live in you, and for you to be enabled to speak in tongues by Him (The Holy Spirit). He is the presence of God in us. Have a minister of the word pray for you to receive Him.

"He shall baptize you with the Holy Ghost, and with fire:" - Matthew 3:11 KJV

"And I will pray the Father, and He shall give you another Comforter, that He may abide with you forever; Even the Spirit of truth; whom the world cannot receive, because it seeth Him not, neither knoweth Him: but ye know Him; for He dwelleth with you, and shall be in you. Yet a little while, and the world seeth me no more; but ye see me: because I live, ye shall live also. At that day ye shall know that I am in my Father, and ye in me, and I in you." - John 14:16-20 KJV

The Holy Spirit is the presence of God the Father, He has a personality and you will know Him.

"But when the Comforter is come, whom I will send unto you from the Father, even the Spirit of truth, which proceedeth from the Father, He shall testify of me:" - John 15:26 KJV

He is the One to make you perceptive from the inside, cause you to understand concepts with no prior learning, and yes, He will reveal to you who Jesus is, through accurate and precise knowledge.

"For the Holy Ghost shall teach you in the same hour what ye ought to say." - Luke 12:12 KJV

"He said unto them, Have ye received the Holy Ghost since ye believed? … 6 And when Paul had laid his hands upon them, the Holy Ghost came on them; and they spake with tongues, and prophesied." - Acts 19:2-6 KJV

"…Receive ye the Holy Ghost:" - John 20:22 KJV

"And they were all filled with the Holy Ghost, and began to speak with other tongues, as the Spirit gave them utterance." - Acts 2:4 KJV

"And when they had prayed, the place was shaken where they were assembled together; and they were all filled with the Holy Ghost, and they spake the word of God with boldness." - Acts 4:31 KJV

"For the kingdom of God is not meat and drink; but righteousness, and peace, and joy in the Holy Ghost." - Romans 14:17 KJV

The Holy Spirit – Prayer and Tongues

Earlier on as I was building on how to get started with doing things differently, strategically using sleeping tablets to ease off and cope with the craving, and moving away from the drug scenes, it is just by a mere human approach, which is good but not enough. The Holy Spirit is Who you need to accomplish your complete recovery. He does the work. Let's dig in.

Who Is The Holy Spirit?

Some Christian denominations don't believe in speaking and praying in tongues as led by the Holy Ghost and this is a big mistake. Some just know the Holy Ghost as part of the Trinity but not His purpose, so they lean only on acknowledging Him to be somewhere. With God, you can't be too picky to suit your need according to your perception. A student choosing to be an engineer can't selectively exclude physics or math because they don't like or understand these subjects, they have to go according to the prescribed course guidelines. So is every principle according to the word in the bible, and God tells us how we ought to live to be victorious.

The Holy Spirit is the presence of God. The Father doesn't leave His throne and walk about to wherever He needs to go or do. The Holy Spirit is that Spirit of God (God Himself) that proceeds from God the Father; hence God's Omnipresence. The Holy Spirit is the Doer of God's work and will.

"Do you not believe that I am in the Father, and that the Father is in Me? What I am telling you I do not say on My own authority and of My own accord; but the Father Who lives continually in Me does the (His) works (His own miracles, deeds of power)." - John 14:10 AMP

Here Jesus was still on earth as a man and was explaining His abilities by the presence of the Father Who is in Him and He in the Father.

"I assure you, most solemnly I tell you (this is a promise), *if anyone steadfastly believes in Me, he will himself be able to do the things that I do; and he will do even greater things than these, because I go to the Father." John 14:12 AMP*

Jesus had to leave so that the Holy Spirit may come down to live in us so that this promise may be fulfilled, that we may even do greater things by the ability of the presence of the Father in us (The Holy Spirit), as it was with Him.

"And I will ask the Father, and He will give you another Comforter (Counselor, Helper, Intercessor, Advocate, Strengthener, and Standby), that He may remain with you forever " - John 14:16 AMP

A Counselor is a Mentor or Psychologist in our terms, he helps you with knowledge about yourself and your mind and workings thereof, to help you in understanding life and thriving and so forth.

A Helper is a Partner who assists you when in need, He serves you.

As an Intercessor, He prays with and for you, and utters words of power (prophesying: speaking forth to be and speaking about the future) on your behalf, to change that which you are not even aware of, and by uttering is when you open your mouth by letting Him speak (tongues – divine language) because your spirit is fused with Him.

As an Advocate He is your Attorney, He speaks on your behalf so that you are not faulted into bondage about law issues, even in the heavenly courts.

He is your Strength. When you feel weak He revitalizes you, He strengthens you in all areas of your life; finances, knowledge, relationships, salvation, health, etc.

As a Standby, when you have run out as a power source would, He kicks in like a standby generator, you never die, and He always boosts you back to life. Scripture says His power is made perfect in my weakness. This is the above Comforter.

"But you will receive power when the Holy Spirit has come upon you, and you will be my witnesses in Jerusalem and all Judea and Samaria, and to the end of the earth." - Acts 1:8 ESV
"That your faith should not stand in the wisdom of men, but in the power of God" - 1 Corinthians 2:5 KJV

This power of God comes by the presence of the Holy Ghost indwelled in you to effect changes for your good according to the will of God for your life – this is the anointing of God in the human body.

"But if the Spirit of Him that raised up Jesus from the dead dwell in you, He that raised up Christ from the dead shall also quicken your mortal bodies by His Spirit that dwelleth in you." - Romans 8:11 KJV

This is the very dynamic power that raised Jesus from the dead and is also able to work for you and speed up all required processes for you too.

"But the fruit of the Spirit is love, joy, peace, longsuffering (endurance)*, gentleness, goodness, faith, meekness, temperance: against such there is no law." Galatians 5:22-23 KJV*

When you are born again you get gifted with these attributes in your spirit. And it is the Holy Spirit that helps you bring them out to the surface and all will be evident of you. You will experience being a loving and caring person as you continue in Christ. You will have this joy that is not dependent on circumstances. When turmoil strikes around you, people will find that you are just as calm even when you don't know what to do. You'd find that you've become this person who just stands the test of time. Kindness and goodness will reign in your life toward others. You will be directed by the Holy Ghost to the word of God and your faith will rise as you hear and understand His ways. And with time you will be patient with even those things you couldn't stand without them affecting your attitude.

"Ye are of God, little children, and have overcome them: because greater is He that is in you, than he that is in the world." With the Holy Spirit in you, you are victorious no doubt. You will not fail.

Jesus told us that all He did was through The Holy Spirit, and there is only one sin that will take you to hell; that is blasphemy against The Holy Spirit. Of which I don't believe any born-again Christian would do.

"And do not grieve the Holy Spirit of God, by whom you were sealed for the day of redemption." - Ephesians 4:30 ESV

Praying in Spirit (Tongues) – By the Holy Spirit

"A time will come, however, indeed it is already here, when the true (genuine) worshipers will worship the Father in spirit and in truth (reality); for the Father is seeking just such people as these as His worshipers. God is a Spirit (a spiritual Being) and those who worship Him must worship Him in spirit and in truth (reality)." - John 4:23-24 AMP

Jesus was explaining to the Samaritan woman at the well when she was being religious about places of worship; saying her forefathers worshiped God at Mount Gerizim but Jews say that Jerusalem is the place where it is necessary and proper to worship God. Jesus guides us here that we are spirits and God is a spirit Being, hence we ought to pray and worship in that realm first before we operate by senses, nor demarcating terrestrial places that are right or wrong to worship. We are that temple where God's presence is. We ought to pray and worship led by the Holy Spirit first. Resonating and returning His word to Himself, our speech being acceptable and guided to Him with assistance by the Holy Spirit. Any person can claim to be good at heart (in spirit), churchgoers, religious people, and sing praises wonderfully so in church – but only humans can perceive goodness through these outward things, however, God sees the heart and that is what He is after.

"For who knows a person's thoughts except the spirit of that person, which is in him? So also no one comprehends the thoughts of God except the Spirit of God." - 1 Corinthians 2:11 ESV

So praying and worshiping in the Holy Ghost is beneficial to us, even when our hearts are not perfect yet, God seeks you who acknowledge and abides or would like to abide by and rely on the power of His Spirit to propel you in worship.

And it is explained in the scriptures that we ought to pray in other tongues being enabled by The Holy Ghost.

"And they were all filled with the Holy Ghost, and began to speak with other tongues, as the Spirit gave them utterance." - Acts 2:4 KJV

Tongues are a gift brought by Him; it is a unique coded utterance that the enemy cannot hear. That is why Satan uses this inexplicable language for man to perceive it as madness because he knows it's a hindrance for him; he can't hear or understand a word. Don't be fooled, Satan doesn't know all things, and neither does he know the future, he only knows the past and present, and he is not all-knowing, he has workers who inform him about occurrences. When you pray or speak in tongues you speak directly with God; you edify, enlighten, and improve yourself to speak forth mysteries. All this has to do with your best interest, circumstance, or someone else's, even giving thanks in worship to God for what He has already done on your behalf without you even perceiving it. The Holy Spirit is the conveyer of God's messages.

"Follow after charity (love), and desire spiritual gifts, but rather that ye may prophesy. For he that **speaketh in an unknown tongue** *speaketh* **not unto men, but unto God**: *for no man understandeth him;* **howbeit in the spirit he speaketh mysteries**. *But he that prophesieth speaketh unto men to edification, and exhortation, and comfort.* **He that speaketh in an unknown tongue edifieth himself;** *but he that prophesieth edifieth the church." 1 Corinthians 14:1-4 KJV*

So you ought to constantly propel yourself in spirit; speaking in tongues every chance you get. In the beginning, it is very unusual and feels awkward, your brain is not accustomed to this, so it will constantly battle with you to stop doing it, but force the utterances to come out of your mouth. You will try to make sense of it, but it is not meant for the human mind to understand, you will not understand it unless you are given the gift of interpretation of tongues after a while, and you will start getting hints on what the Spirit is saying, that is the whole purpose when it comes to God's mysteries. The human mind is susceptible to cheats. You will be like a baby trying to speak the divine language, like a baby trying to say, daddy or mommy, they fumble around their tongue. By forcing themselves to speak they eventually break through in their speech. Start privately speaking in tongues, in the bathroom, or driving, then sooner or later you will gain confidence and it won't matter anymore what people say or think. And commit to going to church as often as you can. There are great blessings associated with the gathering of God's children, and that is where you will learn more about your life in Christ. It must be a bible-based teaching church, where the emphasis is on the Gospel of Christ Jesus.

A prayerful life propels us to victory at any moment, but half the time people don't know how to pray let alone what to pray for. When you pray in tongues (in spirit guided by the Holy Spirit), He knows what you ought to pray for, and you are speaking directly to God and effecting direct supernatural changes for that particular issue. With us, it's all relative when it comes to praying for our needs, often we focus on symptoms. He quickens processes for a progressive change. You are wielding your sword which is your tongue with words of power when praying in tongues.

"But we speak the wisdom of God in a mystery, even the hidden wisdom, which God ordained before the world unto our glory: ... But it is written, Eye hath not seen, nor ear heard, neither have entered into the heart of man, the things which God hath prepared for them that love Him. But God hath revealed them unto us by His Spirit: for the Spirit searcheth all things, yea, the deep things of God. For what man knoweth the things of a man? Even so the things of God knoweth no man, but the Spirit of God. Now we have received, not the spirit of the world, but the Spirit which is of God; that we might know the things that are freely given to us of God. Which things also we speak, not in the words which man's wisdom teacheth, but which the Holy Ghost teacheth; comparing spiritual things with spiritual." - 1 Corinthians 2:7-13 KJV

How to Pray

Let us take a few scriptures to understand the highest authority and power:

"In the beginning was the Word, and the Word was with God, and the Word was God. The same was in the beginning with God. All things were made by Him; and without Him was not any thing made that was made. In Him was life; and the life was the light of men. And the light shineth in darkness; and the darkness comprehended it not ... That was the true Light, which lighteth every man that cometh into the world." - John 1:1-9 KJV

"Who, being in the form of God, thought it not robbery to be equal with God: But made Himself of no reputation, and took upon Him the form of a servant, and was made in the likeness of men: And being found in fashion as a man, He humbled Himself, and became obedient unto death, even the death of the cross. Wherefore God also hath highly exalted Him, and given Him a name which is above every name: That at the name of Jesus every knee should bow, of things in heaven, and things in earth, and things under the earth; And that every tongue should confess that Jesus Christ is Lord, to the glory of the Father." - Philippians 2:6-11 KJV

"Who is the image of the invisible God, the firstborn of every creature: For by Him were all things created, that are in heaven, and that are in earth, visible and invisible, whether they be thrones, or dominions, or principalities, or powers: all things were created by Him, and for Him: And He is before all things, and by Him all things consist. And He is the head of the body, the church: Who is the beginning, the firstborn from the dead; that in all things He might have the pre-eminence. For it pleased the Father that in Him should all fullness dwell; And, having made peace through the blood of His cross, by Him to reconcile all things unto Himself; by Him, I say, whether they be things in earth, or things in heaven." - Colossians 1:15-20 KJV

"I AM Alpha and Omega, the beginning and the ending, …, which is, and which was, and which is to come, the Almighty … Fear not; I AM the first and the last: I Am He that liveth, and was dead; and, behold, I AM alive for evermore, Amen; and have the keys of hell and of death." - Revelation 1:8,17,18 KJV

"And whatsoever ye shall ask in My Name, that will I do, that the Father may be glorified in the Son. If ye shall ask any thing in My Name, I will do it." - John 14:13-14 KJV

It pleased the Father that all the divine fullness (the sum total of the divine perfection, powers, and attributes – the superiority) should dwell in Jesus Christ permanently. And this was through and by the Son's service (finished work of the cross) and intervention of completely reconciling all things back to Himself. And He is the Head of the body; the church, which is us. Firstborn from the dead: Hence being born anew, as we follow suit; *"That their hearts might be comforted, being knit together in love, unto all riches of the full assurance of understanding, to the acknowledgment of the mystery of God, and of the Father, and of Christ; In whom are hid all the treasures of wisdom and knowledge." - Colossians 2:2-3 KJV*

"That I may cause those who love me to inherit [true] riches and that I may fill their treasuries ... Now therefore listen, O you sons; for blessed (happy, fortunate, to be envied) are those who keep my ways ... For whoever finds me [Wisdom] finds life and draws forth and obtains favour from the Lord" - Proverbs 8:21,32,35 AMP

When you find Christ Jesus, you have found Godly Wisdom, because Christ is made wisdom unto us. Ref: 1 Corinthians 1:30

And this was His entire plan from the beginning; God foreknew you and me and had grand designs for us before we were even born.

"For whom He did foreknow, He also did predestinate to be conformed to the image of His Son, that He might be the first born among many brethren. Moreover whom He did predestinate, them He also called: and whom He called, them He also justified: and whom He justified, them He also glorified. What shall we then say to these things? If God be for us, who can be against us? He that spared not His own Son, but delivered Him up for us all, how shall He not with Him also freely give us all things? Who shall lay any thing to the charge of God's elect? It is God that justifieth. Who is he that condemneth? It is Christ that died, yea rather, that is risen again, who is even at the right hand of God, who also maketh intercession for us." - Romans 8:29-34 KJV

Jesus Christ is our High Priest forever after to the order of Melchizedek (Hebrews 6:20). If God spared not His own Son Jesus for our sake, how shall "with Him" also freely give us all things? "And whatsoever ye shall ask in My Name, that will I do".

This is the answer to the confusion when it comes to prayer. Some make Jesus a medium in prayer to God. Yes through and by Him we are saved, however, we don't pray through Jesus. The above scripture gives us insight as He says whatsoever you ask *"in My name,"* that I will do. So when you pray, every request or command you speak, is executed *"in* the name of Jesus," not "through the name". Whatever you are speaking or praying over, should obey the name which is authoritative above every other name, of things in heaven, earth, beneath the earth, things past, present, or future. This Name is the power of attorney granted to you for use. You are ordained to use Jesus' Name.

This is made clear for us to know how to execute commands as an application programmer does when coding software to function correctly. If wrong coding is written or syntax errors are present, the planned outcome for the software will not work. The same concept applies to prayer; hence many don't experience what they pray for.

"Have faith in God. For verily I say unto you, That whosoever shall "say" unto (not talk about, but talk directly to) *this mountain* (issue, challenge), *Be thou removed, and be thou cast into the sea; and shall "not doubt" in his heart, but shall "believe" that those things which he saith shall come to pass; he shall have whatsoever he saith." - Mark 11:22-23 KJV*

This is not for prayer purposes, but for conscious command directed to an issue, or subject. Don't talk about the issue, but talk to the issue itself directly even if unperceivable to the eye. We need to know when to pray, and when to take action according to what we know in faith.

"Therefore I say unto you, What things soever ye desire, when ye pray, believe that ye receive them, and ye shall have them. And when ye stand praying, forgive, if ye have ought against any: that your Father also which is in heaven may forgive you your trespasses." - Mark 11:24 KJV [This refers to prayer]

Let's recollect and put the basics in place as a checklist for effective praying:

- Acknowledge every good thing in you. Be conscious of who you are in Christ
- If any man be in Christ, he "is" a new creation; old things are passed away – You are a new spirit being – You are justified and glorified and in right standing with God
- You function under grace
- Believe – no doubt should be in your heart
- Have Faith in God
- Do not harbor unforgiveness
- There are three levels of creation;
    - Thought, Imagination, and Emotions of Joy attached
    - Words – Speak
    - Action – do what you can do, God will do what you cannot
- Pray and Command in the name of Jesus
- Speak directly to issues – Don't speak about issues
- Receive it in your spirit (heart)
- Give thanks in advance – an indication of your receiving by faith (prayer answered) – faith moves God
- Always remember that God is not a man that He should lie – this helps me personally when doubt tries to creep in
- Praise the Lord as often as you can – Praise always works wonders
- The highest form of prayer is when you pray in thanksgiving – this is faith in action because you are returning God's word to Himself.

- Remember: Do not "want" something; because whatever you say you get - you will be proven to be right – if you "want", it will be a life expedition of wanting which is lack - and this is not finding. i.e. "The Lord is my shepherd; I shall *not want.*" Psalm 23:1

Examples of prayer: degree of effectiveness;
- ✓ Father, I pray that you heal me in Jesus' name Amen

- ✓ Father, I pray that you heal me and I receive my healing in Jesus' name Amen
- ✓ Father, I thank you for all that you have done for me (heartily remind Him about those things you have been pondering on, and can readily remember that which He has done for you); this sickness shall not stay in my body; Jesus was chastised for my peace - I have the peace of God that surpasses all understanding; by the stripes of Jesus I am healed (you are quoting God's word), in the name of Jesus I am healed (touch your body and boldly declare): body, be healed; The same Spirit that raised Jesus from the dead lives in me and Is revitalizing every fibre of my being now in Jesus' Name Amen! (what you are saying and reflecting is acknowledging the power of the Holy Spirit and His presence, here you are stirring divinity in you, exercising power and authority over sickness)

God is loving, merciful, and consistent. He always steps in to intervene even when you don't know how to do things. This might be any of the numerous reasons why you lack understanding; you might cry out to Him simply expressing a need for healing, then get relieved from your ailment without any of these protocols I'm referring to. But more often, the same ailment returns because you might not be aware that you are the cause of it, and you keep doing the same flaw repeatedly. This can be any aspect of your life. However He doesn't cease to help, the only issue is that some don't know how to listen to or recognize His voice. He is that gentle voice speaking on the inside of you, but at times we are too busy to hear. God is dynamic in His communication, He will use any possible way to get your attention, and all you have to do is be intentional in thinking of Him each moment of every day and then take notice of His prompting in your spirit.

Here's a quick guide when it comes to personal awareness and growth to help in your prayer points for the re-creation of self.

- Make time for you and God alone
- Ask yourself who you are currently, and who you wish to be
- Make up your mind, be firm, and agree within on your future self
- Pull the future self to the now. This will activate conflicting notions; beliefs, ideas, and emotions about why you can't be that which you imagine. This is good because now you will see the real causes (beliefs, ideas, and mindset) of what led you to your current self, then reiterate, see, and feel your future. Echo this daily and put pressure to override old memories by creating a new you.
- Analyse thoughts that dominantly occupy your mind and separate them according to your preference, into those that serve you and those that don't. If you are not happy with the current state, it means the thought process must change. Doing the same things over and over hoping for change is madness. It's not easy but you must do it. These are just residues left from your past, and we must get rid of them. I also feel that I'm writing to myself.

- Accept what you have currently become, and bless the experience, it has brought you to some understanding and revelation about the experience. Then you will have peace when you see things for what they are with no blame attached – Though it's not preferable, sometimes you are first to become that which you are not to be, so you know and understand what not to do or be when you are who you ought to be. The Apostle Paul knew who he was as Saul of Tarsus the tormentor of Christians before the road to Damascus.

- See the thoughts, words, actions, and experiences you wish for as the new you.
- Renew your mind with the word of God; this is your spiritual food. You are reversing the process: society, environment, and the world has fed your senses (body), your body fed your soul, and your soul fed you (spirit). Now, You (spirit) must feed (by God's word) your soul (cleansing), and your soul will remember who you really are, and will dictate rules and functions to your body (senses) about your new estate's preferred lifestyle - way of life. The body is generally stubborn, hence you ought to be conscious of the grace you have, your gift of righteousness, and the love of God for you. You are born to win; you were predetermined to match the likeness of Christ.
- Stay in the Word and never waiver, so that you know how to pray and when not to pray but utter commands.
- Purposefully worship God and sing praises even if you think you can't sing.
- And please, get acquainted with the Holy Spirit and know Him; He is the best Friend you can ever have!

Let me clarify this command-action business when I say there is a time not to pray. A few illustrations might shed light.

When a problem impacts you unprepared, you might struggle with it because your weapons are not and have not been in place. Creation, Re-Creation, Manifestation, and Birth of an Entity, an Idea, or Matter, are largely favored by preparation; nature doesn't favor premature production quite much, hence the usual struggle with things birthed or created rashly. By preparation, you get to understand the dynamics and the heart of the matter, and by meditating on the matter, the universe works together for the matter to be revealed or it reveals itself to you for a consensus (you know that light bulb moment for instance? It's not in the physical) so that you get an understanding about it. Then you get an opportunity to state your case to the matter, maybe you would like for it to go away; matter has intelligence, so it will understand that it is not welcome anymore even if it was brought there by your own choice it has to leave. That energy would have to obey the rules of the game. If it is anger, for instance, the matter will be revealed and explained to you what it is and how this entity has come about, then it has to leave. Sometimes it is a matter unawares you seek; with me, it was once peace, and when it was revealed, it took me a short while to realize that this was what I was looking for, then God explained to me the reason I was being the way I was. The same thing goes for a lack in one's life, sickness, demon possessions, riches, and so forth. However this is mostly for those who like to know how things work as I do, but it doesn't have to be this way. God favors all of us, and it's generally easy for those who wouldn't bother themselves with these mechanics that get results quickly, it is much faith in itself.

Jesus spent lots of time in prayer and communion with the Father first before going about executing his business; healing and all. He often didn't pray for people but issued out commands to demons and situations. He was always prepared, full of wisdom and comprehension about matters.

When the Egyptian army had cornered the Israelites by the Red Sea, it was a sure win for them. Surely the commanders were like look at these fools, how far did they think they were going to run. Then Moses started to contemplate praying to the Father (It was a bit late, the army was very near). God said no! No praying! Lift up your rod and split the waters, so he did and they escaped. God didn't split the sea, Moses did, and by this time he recognized and remembered his anointing. He was the anointed of God, and like Jesus said we will do greater things than He did. God could have easily killed that army Himself earlier, but He always desires for us to know what we are capable of.

He is an extraordinary strategist. Look what happened with Joshua when the Israelites were to invade the promised land. The majority of the Israeli spies came back with a report that they were grasshoppers in comparison to the inhabitants of the land who were giants. The land was also surrounded and protected by a great wall. God told Joshua to see that He has given Jericho into his hands; the king thereof, and the mighty men of valor. He gave Joshua instructions on what to do to achieve that goal. Joshua told the Israelites to go around the city once a day for six days, and seven times on the seventh day. They were to keep quiet as they did this, not a word out of their lips. Not that they were creeping because surely the inhabitants saw them outside, but they were to follow specific instructions. On the seventh day, Joshua told them the last part of the instruction. Which was for the nation to shout out loud when instructed. They did and the great wall fell flat. Joshua 6.

The lesson behind the strategy reveals that humans like to rationalize things according to their understanding: Joshua was a man of God and relied not on his own understanding, but on God's. Should he have explained to his people what the whole plan was, hell would have broken loose; "You think this enormous wall will fall because of noise? Mind you making us walk around the whole city for seven days? You must be foolish!". This is the limited human sense - logic speaking.

A similar event happened with King Jehoshaphat when word came that there was a great army coming to attack him. He consulted with the prophet of God and then prayed. He was instructed on what to do and not to be afraid nor discouraged by this imminent attack; for the battle is not his, but God's. The King settled and believed in the prophet of God. He appointed singers to be at the battle forefront to praise the Lord and instructed them to sing: "Praise the Lord, for His mercy endureth forever." Then later, without fighting, Jehoshaphat and his people discovered that their enemies fought and destroyed one another through confusion and madness. He found an abundance of riches among the dead bodies. 2 Chronicles chapter 20.

Not all battles are yours either. Praising God in times of need demonstrates your faith in Him. You need a man of God to guide you in your life, and you find them in church. Heeding and surrendering yourself to instructions can yield surprising results. This is exercising wisdom.

Seek Knowledge and Wisdom, and God will grant it to you.

"The Lord formed and brought Me [Wisdom] forth at the beginning of His way, before His acts of old. I [Wisdom] was inaugurated and ordained from everlasting, from the beginning, before ever the earth existed." Proverbs 8:22-23 AMP

Don't Be Sin Conscious – Be Righteousness Conscious

"For if by one man's offence death reigned by one; much more they which receive abundance of grace and of the gift of righteousness shall reign in life by one, Jesus Christ. Therefore as by the offence of one judgment came upon all men to condemnation; even so by the righteousness of one the free gift came upon all men unto justification of life. For as by one man's disobedience many were made sinners, so by the obedience of one shall many be made righteous." - Romans 5:17-19 KJV

God's unconditional love, as His unmerited favor (grace) for people to live by, is revealed between two timelines; at creation, and the birth of Jesus Christ to the now. In between the creation of man and Jesus, the Law of Moses (the ten commandments) was established due to the pollution and corruption of humankind (sin). Humans made choices that led to their own demise obliviously so. These types of self-destructive behavioral patterns become a norm after a while. Even when the Israelites were taken out of slavery from the Egyptians and were on a journey in the wilderness, they were still moaning and groaning, complaining all the time about this and that, but God demonstrated grace and provided for them. As the scripture says; the Law was like a schoolmaster being established for those that didn't understand how they should lead their lives.
Galatians chapter 3 AMPC:

"O YOU poor and silly and thoughtless and unreflecting and senseless Galatians! Who has fascinated or bewitched or cast a spell over you, unto whom-right before your very eyes-Jesus Christ (the Messiah) was openly and graphically set forth and portrayed as crucified?

Let me ask you this one question: Did you receive the [Holy] Spirit as the result of obeying the Law and doing its works, or was it by hearing [the message of the Gospel] and believing [it]? [Was it from observing a law of rituals or from a message of faith?]

Are you so foolish and so senseless and so silly? Having begun [your new life spiritually] with the [Holy] Spirit, are you now reaching perfection [by dependence] on the flesh?

Have you suffered so many things and experienced so much all for nothing (to no purpose)-if it really is to no purpose and in vain?

Then does He Who supplies you with His marvelous [Holy] Spirit and works powerfully and miraculously among you do so on [the grounds of your doing] what the Law demands, or because of your believing in and adhering to and trusting in and relying on the message that you heard?

Thus Abraham believed in and adhered to and trusted in and relied on God, and it was reckoned and placed to his account and credited as righteousness (as **conformity to the divine will in purpose, thought, and action***). [Gen. 15:6.]*

Know and understand that it is [really] the people [who live] by faith who are [the true] sons of Abraham.

And the Scripture, foreseeing that God would justify (declare righteous, put in right standing with Himself) the Gentiles in consequence of faith, proclaiming the Gospel [foretelling the glad tidings of a Savior long beforehand] to Abraham in the promise, saying, In you shall all the nations [of the earth] be blessed. [Gen.12:3.]

So then, those who are people of faith are blessed and made happy and favoured by God [as partners in fellowship] with the believing and trusting Abraham.

And all who depend on the Law [who are seeking to be justified by obedience to the Law of rituals] are under a curse and doomed to disappointment and destruction, for it is written in the Scriptures, Cursed (accursed, devoted to destruction, doomed to eternal punishment) be everyone who does not continue to abide (live and remain) by all the precepts and commands written in the Book of the Law and to practice them. [Deut. 27:26.]

Now it is evident that no person is justified (declared righteous and brought into right standing with God) through the Law, for the Scripture says, The man in right standing with God [the just, the righteous] shall live by and out of faith and he who through and by faith is declared righteous and in right standing with God shall live. [Hab. 2:4.]

But the Law does not rest on faith [does not require faith, has nothing to do with faith], for it itself says, He who does them [the things prescribed by the Law] shall live by them [not by faith]. [Lev.18:5.]

Christ purchased our freedom [redeeming us] from the curse (doom) of the Law [and its condemnation] by [Himself] *becoming a curse for us, for it is written [in the Scripture], Cursed is everyone who hangs on a tree (is crucified); [Deut. 21:23.]*

To the end that through [their receiving] Christ Jesus, the blessing [promised] to Abraham might come upon the Gentiles, so that we through faith might [all] receive [the realization of] the promise of the [Holy] Spirit.

To speak in terms of human relations, brethren, [if] even a man makes a last will and testament (a merely human covenant), no one sets it aside or makes it void or adds to it when once it has been drawn up and signed (ratified, confirmed).

Now the promises (covenants, agreements) were decreed and made to Abraham and his Seed (his Offspring, his Heir). He [God] does not say, And to seeds (descendants, heirs), as if referring to many persons, but, And to your Seed (your Descendant, your Heir), obviously referring to one individual, Who is [none other than] Christ (the Messiah). [Gen.13:15;17:8.]

This is my argument: **The Law, which began 430 years after the covenant [concerning the coming of Messiah], does not and cannot annul the covenant previously established (ratified) by God, so as to abolish the promise and make it void. [Exod. 12:40.]**

For if the inheritance [of the promise depends on observing] the Law [as these false teachers would like you to believe], it no longer [depends] on the promise; however, God gave it to Abraham [as a free gift solely] by virtue of His promise.

What then was the purpose of the Law? It was later added [later on, after the promise, to disclose and expose to men their guilt] because of transgressions and [to make men more conscious of the sinfulness] of sin; and it was intended to be in effect until the Seed (the Descendant, the Heir) should come, to and concerning Whom the promise had been made. And it [the Law] was arranged and ordained and appointed through the instrumentality of angels [and was given] by the hand (in person) of a go-between [Moses, an intermediary person between God and man].

Now a go-between (intermediary) has to do with and implies more than one party [there can be no mediator with just one person]. Yet God is [only] one Person [and He was the sole party in giving that promise to Abraham. But the Law was a contract between two, God and Israel; its validity was dependent on both].

Is the Law then contrary and opposed to the promises of God? Of course not! For if a Law had been given which could confer [spiritual] life, then righteousness and right standing with God would certainly have come by Law.

But the Scriptures [picture all mankind as sinners] shut up and imprisoned by sin, so that [the inheritance, blessing] which was promised through faith in Jesus Christ (the Messiah) might be given (released, delivered, and committed) to [all] those who believe [who adhere to and trust in and rely on Him].

Now before the faith came, we were perpetually guarded under the Law, kept in custody in preparation for the faith that was destined to be revealed (unveiled, disclosed),

So that the Law served [to us Jews] as our trainer [our guardian, our guide to Christ, to lead us] until Christ [came], that we might be justified (declared righteous, put in right standing with God) by and through faith.

But now that the faith has come, we are no longer under a trainer (the guardian of our childhood).

For in Christ Jesus you are all sons of God through faith.

For as many [of you] as were baptized into Christ [into a spiritual union and communion with Christ, the Anointed One, the Messiah] have put on (clothed yourselves with) Christ.
There is [now no distinction] neither Jew nor Greek, there is neither slave nor free, there is not male and female; for you are all one in Christ Jesus.
And if you belong to Christ [are in Him Who is Abraham's Seed], then you are Abraham's offspring and [spiritual] heirs according to promise.

You then ought to say with conviction and confidence; "I am not cursed, but I am blessed" when you understand the above passage.

This right standing you have with God is by His favor, you did not earn it and you can never earn it. The Jews stood and lived by the law, but could not accomplish obedience to the law. The law came only to show up man's behavior and to guide him. Does this mean that we have to disobey the 10 commandments? Definitely not! James 2:10 explains that if you obey all the laws but one, you are guilty of all of them. Further study of Galatians reveals to us that when you are not acquainted with and understand God, you are in bondage of sin. But when you understand and are acquainted with God, you can never go back to your old ways where you are controlled by worthless standards of living. Hence Jesus said that we should love God with all our hearts, and love one another, for if we do this, it is unlikely to harm the next person. You cannot present yourself holy to God even at your highest esteemed feeling of goodness.

Amid our shortcomings and unsavory habits, God says we are righteous. He affirms that we must live by faith. "…now that the faith has come, we are no longer under a trainer (the guardian of our childhood)" which is the law, but in Christ Jesus by faith.

God calls things that are not as though they were, and you get the understanding of this when you realize He doesn't live in time and space and He's not bound by this, He only created this for us. In the context of sin, He knows why sin cannot have dominion over you if you are in Christ. And He says we ought to imitate Him. So you must see yourself as He says you are because you are the finished product as He has created you as ideal as He saw fit in His sight. Use your imagination, the creative power within your grasp to create or recreate your future according to His plan for your life. What you have constantly seen and spoken about in the past has led you to where you are today, this is evident that your constant imagination backed by your words manifests in your life, so get in the right and perfect will of God for your life and see wonderful things gravitating into your life experience.

When you believe what God says about your right standing with Him, and you confess that you are the righteousness of God, you will start seeing your fruits, actions, or behavior changing for the better with no effort at all; right living will be a result. It doesn't matter when you falter, these are just residues from your past falling away, it's only a matter of time till people will be amazed at how you've changed for the better.

The body and your spirit man will always be in contrast till perfection is achieved.

There will come a point where it will be easy to do right, but hard to do something wrong (sinning), unlike how it used to be easy to do wrong things [by purposefully positioning your mindset and speech in what the word says; setting yourself up for success: constantly uplifting your self-worth and speaking of good things to come as though they already are].

"For sin shall not have dominion over you: for ye are not under the law, but under grace." - Romans 6:14 KJV

When you are born again, you live under the grace of God, not by our efforts to earn points with Him. Righteousness is a gift, and you can never buy a gift, it comes free because He loves us.

"Finally, brethren, whatsoever things are true, whatsoever things are honest, whatsoever things are just, whatsoever things are pure, whatsoever things are lovely, whatsoever things are of a good report; if there be any virtue, and if there be any praise, think on these things." - Philippians 4:8 KJV

Do What You Can Do – God Will Do What You Can't

Secrets and rebellion hinder progress to our divinely ordained destinies, which is why we ought to testify about our victories when God helps us to conquer issues and circumstances in our lives. Some people love God secretly, and yes He is a patient and loving Father, He knows the steps and processes we have to be elevated to in time from lack of knowledge some have. However, none of us fancy being a secret lover in a relationship, this translates to insignificance to the one kept secret. The enemy knows the effectiveness and power in acknowledging the presence of God in one's life and openly so, and the ineffectiveness thereof when otherwise. It is reason enough why many perish even when they know in their hearts that God exists. The thoughts and intentions of the heart are not enough to get us through. The enemy bombards you with thoughts to be sin conscious, then you say what will people think, they will say I am a hypocrite, I don't even want to lie to myself, and I don't even like hypocrites. As I said earlier, you delve and give sustainable reason to a lie you initially bought without even knowing the true will of the Father or His word.

This is how the enemy has lied and kept many in bondage for so many years. Normally, with drugs, many think if people can't find out, then I'm fine. The more you are able to keep it this way, the more you think of yourself as clever or skillful, but you see, this is another lie the enemy feeds you and makes you feel untouchable in what you are concealing. Then he later says, should they find out they will use it against you. However, it is the deeper you get into his clutches of burden, which is why your heart feels condemned; it is not God that condemns, but that foul spirit that feels condemned within you. One gets clouded from within by these entities, you feel like it is you who is being condemned. Foul spirits can breed frustration to a point where one loses their mind and cannot identify their true self or thoughts.

Take for instance vows taken by gangsters, should someone from the outside insult their member, the whole gang would feel offended as if it was directed specifically to them because they have vowed to be one but in respect, they are separate entities. We are generally not aware of such spiritual activities as they are hidden from the naked eye's view. We ought to be trained to discern evil from good.

I was once involved in a life of crime in my early teenage years, and this is another story of the misguided use of faith and belief. I believed that I could do anything I set my heart to, but this criminal mindset was influenced by my environment of cause and the powers thereof. I theoretically learned and meditated on everything illegal that I was about to do. I started alone, and these moments were intense, I would sit alone, plan and envision what I was about to do; be it contemplating car theft, mag-wheels, sound systems, or fraud. And I would go and commit the act exactly how I imagined it. It *felt* good when I did this, I didn't know what faith was then, nor really grasped the meaning of believing. I was fourteen when I started with car accessories, then the first car I stole I was fifteen. I drove around my neighborhood all night till the early hours of the morning till I realized I had school later on then ditched the vehicle. It was all in secret from the moment I started. I had to be secret about it because I had a very strict uncle whom I love dearly and was a big part of my life, and I was under his roof at the time. The more I stole, the more confident I got and the more deceptive I got. Word got around as I dealt with stolen goods, but I wasn't aware of this till one of my close friends came and told me that he heard about what I do and he wants me to teach him because he needs the money. I felt for the guy because I knew his family background so I did. But you see the enemy was aware of what my grandmother had taught and instilled in me, prayer, but I didn't really know the power of it. From an early age she taught me Psalm 23 "The Lord is my shepherd I shall not want …" and we would pray every night before bedtime and every morning. My first experience and awareness of understanding what achievement is was in my primary school days when I got my report card and I was the best in my class. This had a huge impact on my grandmother and I saw the joy in her eyes. This was my motivation to do well in class just to see her smile. The more I did well, the more I could feel the joy and pride she had in me, and this overcame her sorrow of lack in the family. I remember I would be taking those long walks to and from school imagining and speaking under my breath that that year I'll be number one again in class. And so it was, but from standard six (now grade 8) I started having other ideas, that money solves issues in life so I have to secretly make a plan. But of cause, this was the voice of the enemy destructing me from what I was to become. Later it became evident who I had become. It was cool to be liked in the underworld, that you are the discreet lad the old G's like working with and you can do the job. Guys thought twice before they would step to me, the girls liked my style, grandma had food on the table, I was in the top ten in class, and the future couldn't look brighter. But the cookie was about to crumble. This is what the enemy does, he is the father of all lies, and he is the king of destruction. He will lie and give you an idea to counteract what you don't like at a particular moment, and generally, we get the warning bells, but he will reinstate the lie by supporting false evidence and having you focus on the problem day to day, to be short sited and having a now mentality. I wasn't praying anymore except when in jail or in trouble. God would answer my prayers and get me out of trouble, and I would steal again, and He would rescue me again, on and on it went. But you see He was my secret lover; I was ashamed to mention it to any of my friends then because at this age my thinking was wise guys don't talk about God, we don't entertain soft things.

So here were the aspects that were influencing my life unwittingly: I had too little knowledge even about prayer, and now I wasn't praying at all accordingly, I wasn't imagining good things anymore but the wrong kind. My tongue wasn't speaking enriching words of power for charting the right course for my life but speaking ungodly swear words. The company I kept mostly misguided me, fools leading fools, I had entertained anger and imagined all sorts of retaliation that my aura and demeanor had changed. Being fierce was the order of the day, my actions were led by envy to acquire what I saw others had. The sense of greatness is temporarily lived. I lived a secretive double standard life even though I had this yearning to explore knowledge and other people who inspired me positively so; if they found out I would feel ashamed. I couldn't get myself to quit even if I wanted to. What will the crowd in my world think! But God's mercies are endless, His grace is sufficient. One constant friend told me I should go for a job interview he had heard about. At the time there was a war going on inside of me, but God gave me the courage. See if you get the job. Only when you start yielding yourself to Him things will start moving in the spirit realm for your betterment.

It was a transformation period in South Africa, and the company I went to for an interview, was rife with racism. I passed the interview, they sent me for a medical check and the report came back that I wasn't fit for the job, my urine had blood in it and I mustn't come for the job. Then my attitude and stubbornness kicked in, I forced my case, gave them a piece of my mind, and said I will come for the job. I met all the requirements they wanted, and the blood story was an excuse, they were being biased and segregated by color. I was fit and felt competent for the job. The racial issues just forced me to get a place there. However in all honesty I couldn't see myself being a technician going house to house around my neighborhood announcing to my peers that I am a broken man who has resorted to fixing telephones, with no prospects of becoming rich, that I had no courage anymore to be a G. Nevertheless I got the job. I dealt with the silly scorns from time to time from friends in the townships. Word got around that I don't have the courage anymore I'm now the working class. But slowly I got lifted by the compliments I got from old folks thanking me for fixing their telephones, being chosen in the office at work to work on bigger projects, and being on a specialized team. God was working behind the scene and I wasn't aware still.

At this moment the bondage of the secret life had no power over me anymore; the secret came to light, and my misconceptions of the pride of life were destroyed. I learned new things, and a new way of life: darkness cannot stand the light, even scientifically. When you shine a light in a dark room, it becomes light, and this is a lesser truth.

All these things I was blind to. Only by the grace of God and fellowship with Him does He point out as I ask Him questions on my journey to understand, and this is only when you are true to yourself and spend time with Him alone [(self-introspect) to know yourself you must know your Father. Hence we walk around chasing not knowing what we are looking for. But it is our souls' yearning and trying to tell us who we are].

I remember reading one of our pastor's articles on the subconscious and knowings thereof; that the soul of a man knows everything, no matter how unknowledgeable you might think you are, it is just dormant, your consciousness is bombarding it with worldly information, hence when revelation knowledge comes is like you are awoken from a deep sleep, like being awoken from a drunken state and you become enlightened and aware of this wonderful world you belong and live from. That when you intimately seek answers to something you are directed to and the answer is also directed towards you in a profound manner that is almost inexplicable. When you realize it, you are never alone as much as you think. You are made of love, and love can never exist outside a relationship.

Another insert was from this other book stating that man cannot live his life to its fullness and with joy when he doesn't believe or think that he is loved. It's like a bird that has its wings clipped off, it will only hop on the ground being miserable because it is in its nature and design to fly. So with man, it is in his nature and design to be in love, you cannot exist properly without love because God is love and saw it good that He created you, even in His image and likeness. So you are love and should operate as love should. You cannot separate yourself from yourself, only God can, and it was the love He had for you for Him to do that. When man fell from grace, God saw it fit that He should be devoid of part of Himself for yours and mine's sake that He might come and live as a man of flesh and blood that He might return our glory to its original estate.

He made us rulers and we were fooled, but He did not leave it at that, He restored our kingship for us. But many don't know this, hence it is important to know; lack of knowledge is not bliss. When many are in trouble, they think God has left them. He never leaves, we just turn our focus away from Him and focus on problems, hence we have it on record for our study in understanding this principle flesh and blood has accustomed itself to. In the bible; as Jesus was fully man, at the cross when he cried "Lord God why have you left me?," it was 'Jesus the man' that lost sight of God the Father, when all sin, past, present, and future were laid upon him who knew no sin, for you and me. All 'the Man' saw and felt was the pain, but that same Spirit that raised Him from the dead (The Presence of The Father, The Holy Ghost) was always right there beside him but He couldn't perceive God to be there – that's what happens when you focus on problems, you magnify the pain. But Jesus didn't give in, He finished the work. He resurrected victoriously, He collected all the keys of hell and of death, and restoration was done. He had nothing similar to the devil, the devil couldn't refuse but to give back what he had stolen. An abundance of grace and the gift of righteousness (right standing with God) were dispersed to mankind to rule again as kings in this world. And sin shall not have dominion over you or me. Nothing shall separate us from the love of Christ. NOTHING! Not drugs, not thievery, not lies, not trials, not failure.

Nothing can, and it is like that, my friend. What I want to highlight from my experience above is the truth God tells about His people perishing due to lack of knowledge. When Christ Jesus says in -

Matthew 18:3 KJV *"Verily I say unto you, Except ye be converted, and become as little children, ye shall not enter into the kingdom of heaven."*

My grandmother grounded and shared with me the little she knew about God, but that sufficed for me then. I was on the right path. Children do not complicate matters; it wasn't a need for me to want to know how things work like I later did. I walked around alone kicking stones confessing the right words and focusing on the result I envisioned. It comes to mind also how often I picked up money from nowhere and took it home. Only now do I recognize that I was believing and exercising my faith unwittingly. This is the presence of the Father in one's life, even when you don't know it. And yes Jesus does state that we have to be converted and become like little children; beyond the literal consciousness to humbling yourself to be obedient, is the further truth of being born again, because this means your spirit is recreated and as a spirit man you are, you become a newborn baby in the spirit in the kingdom of God.

"Therefore if any man be in Christ, he is a new creature (creation)*: old things are passed away; behold* (see)*, all things are become new." - 2 Corinthians 5:17*

When you have chosen to accept and confess Jesus as your Lord and Saviour and choose to live a new life, you consequently become humble and the humility will surface because you are now like Christ. It's only a matter of time before this is evident.

These are attributes we see in little children; faith-works. A little boy will tell you that no one is greater than his dad. But then when you grow up and become knowledgeable, you want to lean on your understanding, else it is nonsense to you because you aren't clear about things or have certain acquired contrary beliefs. This is very risky when it comes to spiritual growth; pride prevents you from learning and knowing more, for you think you know better.

"Let no man deceive himself. If any man among you seemeth to be wise in this world, let him become a fool, that he may be wise. For it is written, He taketh the wise in their own craftiness. And again, The Lord knoweth the thoughts of the wise, that they are vain." - 1 Corinthians 3:18-20 KJV

"For the story and message of the cross is sheer absurdity and folly to those who are perishing and on their way to perdition, but to us who are being saved it is the [manifestation of] the power of God.

For it is written, I will baffle and render useless and destroy the learning of the learned and the philosophy of the philosophers and the cleverness of the clever and the discernment of the discerning; I will frustrate and nullify [them] and bring [them] to nothing.

Where is the wise man (the philosopher)? Where is the scribe (the scholar)? Where is the investigator (the logician, the debater) of this present time and age? Has not God shown up the nonsense and folly of this world's wisdom?

For when the world with all its earthly wisdom failed to perceive and recognize and know God by means of its own philosophy, God in His wisdom was pleased through the foolishness of preaching [salvation, procured by Christ and to be had through Him], to save those who believed (who clung to and trusted in and relied on Him).

For while Jews [demandingly] ask for signs and miracles and Greeks pursue philosophy and wisdom, We preach Christ (the Messiah) crucified, [preaching which] to the Jews is a scandal and an offensive stumbling block [that springs a snare or trap], and to the Gentiles it is absurd and utterly unphilosophical nonsense.

But to those who are called, whether Jew or Greek (Gentile), Christ [is] the Power of God and the Wisdom of God. [This is] because the foolish thing [that has its source in] God is wiser than men, and weak thing [that springs] from God is stronger than men.

For [simply] consider your own call, brethren; not many [of you were considered to be] wise according to human estimates and standards, nor many influential and powerful, not many of high and noble birth. [No] for God selected (deliberately chose) what in the world is foolish to put the wise to shame, and what the world calls weak to put the strong to shame. And God also selected (deliberately chose) what in the world is lowborn and insignificant and branded and treated with contempt, even the things that are nothing, that He might depose and bring to nothing the things that are, So that no mortal man should [have pretense for glorifying and] boast in the presence of God. But it is from Him that you have your life in Christ Jesus, Whom God made our Wisdom from God, [revealed to us a knowledge of the divine plan of salvation previously hidden, manifesting itself as] our Righteousness [thus making us upright and putting us in right standing with God], and our Consecration [making us pure and holy], and our Redemption [providing our ransom from eternal penalty for sin]. So then, as it is written, Let him who boasts and proudly rejoices and glories, boast and proudly rejoice and glory in the Lord." - 1 Corinthians 1:18-31 AMP

Even youngsters don't listen to their parents when heeded of something thinking they know it all.

Ephesians 6:1-2 AMP says *"Children, obey your parents in the Lord [as His representatives], for it is just and right. Honor (esteem and value as precious) your father and your mother-this is the first commandment with a promise- [Exodus 20:12] That all may be well with you and that you may live long on the earth."* Exodus 20:12 says *"Regard (treat with honor, due obedience, and courtesy) your father and mother, that your days may be long in the land the Lord your God gives you."*

We can see the indication in the above scriptures to what causes most of our problems in life or to the point of premature deaths without even knowing what has influenced such; " …that all may be well with you …" hence we sometimes see the difference in the same class of people, some evidently things running smoothly for them in life and we label them lucky, contrary to their peers who just seem to hit a brick wall after the next. " …and that you may live long on the earth." It is heartbreaking when a

114

parent has to bury their beloved child, every parent wishes to see their child grow up and become a responsible parent themselves and turn their parents into grandparents. Unfortunately, there are more premature deaths than we could comprehend due to a lack of understanding. It is important to take caution.

It was not only to make truths harder to understand mysteries when Jesus shared in parables; but so that those who don't have the heart to hear will not receive the glorious truths that God has. This was through the constant rejection of Jesus Christ that he started teaching in parables.

"Do not give that which is holy (the sacred thing) to the dogs, and do not throw your pearls before hogs, lest they trample upon them with their feet and turn and tear you in pieces." - Matthew 7:6

God refuses to teach or open His ways to the unteachable; men of pride. Make sure whatever sacred thing you give to someone that they are worth it.

Here is a divine obligation: *God says if you should see (His word), and you should hear (His word) and understand (His word); then He is obliged to heal you.* No buts about it.

Matthew 13:14-15 Jesus explains the parable of the Sower *"Because it is given unto you (His disciples) to know the mysteries of the kingdom of heaven, but to them (those who deliberately refuse the word of God) it is not given. For whosoever hath (a hearing heart; deliberately wanting to hear and learn even if initially they don't understand) to him shall be given, and he shall have more abundance: but whosoever hath not (doesn't have a hearing heart, deliberately refusing the word of God) from him shall be taken away even that he hath. Therefore speak I to them in parables: because they seeing see not; and hearing they hear not, neither do they understand. And in them (those who deliberately refuse the word of God) is fulfilled the prophecy of Esaias, which saith, By hearing ye shall hear, and shall not understand; and seeing ye shall see, and shall not perceive: For this people's heart is waxed gross (oily heart), and their ears are dull of* *hearing (heavy ears), and their eyes they have closed (purposefully refusing to see); lest at any time they should see with their eyes, and hear with their ears, and should understand with their heart, and should be converted, <u>and I should heal them</u>."*

I always rely on a reminder that God is not a man that He should lie to me; He has nothing to gain from me. And His word has proven itself to me over and over again. *Proverbs 22:20-27 says "My son, attend to my words; incline thine ear unto my sayings. Let them not depart from thine eyes; keep them in the midst of thine heart. For they are life unto those that find them, <u>and health to all their flesh</u>".*

So it is wise to deliberately seek, see, and hear even when you don't understand the word of God because He knows better and His word is sharper than any two-edged sword; it discerns the intentions of your heart.

Feed on the word of God, because when you are born again as you are a spirit being, you ought to eat spiritual food which is the word itself, to make you grow into maturity. This is what Jesus meant when He was tempted by the devil to turn stones into bread when Jesus was hungry from fasting; that man shall not live by bread alone (you are not your body – bread is only for your vessel's sustenance), but by every "word" that proceeded from the mouth of God. It starts as milk for infants in the Lord, then to meaty food of the word; these are deeper truths and mysteries of operations of the divine where you function from.

As Paul was indicating the stage the Corinthians were in maturity, that they were immature babies in the Lord (and there is nothing wrong with babies, but they have to grow, they mustn't remain that way): *"However brethren, I could not talk to you as to spiritual [men], but as to nonspiritual [men of the flesh, in whom the carnal nature predominates], as to mere infants [in the new life] in Christ [unable to talk yet!] I fed you with milk, not solid food, for you were not yet strong enough [to be ready for it]; but even yet you are not strong enough [to be ready for it], For you are still [unspiritual, having the nature] of the flesh [under the control of ordinary impulses]. For as long as [there are] envying and jealousy and wrangling and factions among you, are you not unspiritual and of the flesh, behaving yourselves after a human standard and like mere [unchanged] men? ... 16 Do you not discern and understand that you [the whole church at Corinth] are God's temple [His sanctuary][ref: 1 Corinthians 6:17] "But he that is joined unto the Lord is one spirit" and that God's Spirit has His permanent dwelling in you [to be at home in you, collectively as a church and also individually]? 18 Let no person deceive himself. If anyone among you supposes that he is wise in this age, let him become a fool [let him discard his worldly discernment and recognize himself as dull, stupid and foolish, without true learning and scholarship], that he may become [really] wise."*

I appreciate it when God reprimands and shows me my foolishness because He always follows up with a solution. This shows that He is not scornful, but interested in my development.

God's love for us is amazing, the more you find out the more you wish you could understand further, but many blame him for misfortunes that are unfounded because they know not. Should you pursue Him and ask genuine questions, He will comfort you and show up in your time of need.

So the real reason I'm writing to you isn't much about my teenage life, that's another story altogether, but an episode in my adult life I had put myself in, even after learning a bit more about God.

Just when you think you got a few things figured out and life seems better, you tend to get a bit loose and entertain and reminisce about good old times and try things out to be pleasing to colleagues or friends. Then the enemy strikes without you knowing. Be consistent in the word to be reminded of who you are and build up.

This time I had chosen to live right, old things were done. I was in a steady relationship with a God-fearing lady, my now wife. It all started at this accounting firm I was working at, a new environment with high expectations, excuse the pun. But I didn't know that I was in for a life-altering experience when I tried my first line of cocaine. Another thing you must know is the devil is persistent, and you must be persistent with your salvation.

Keep him at bay at all times. Even when he couldn't win Jesus with his temptations in the wilderness to divert Him from fulfilling God's purpose for us, the bible tells us that he left Him for a season to return later. This time in a different way, in one of His disciples; when Jesus was revealing for the first time to His disciples the Father's plan that He would suffer and die. Then Peter called Him to the side to speak to Him privately that this shouldn't happen, then Jesus said to him get thee behind me Satan. Peter wasn't Satan, but Satan was using Peter to tempt Jesus again.

I was tempted and fell for it, and had many years of tribulations. I do not want to write about the whole experience of taking drugs and how I felt because all that I felt and thought were all lies. However, this is just to point out lessons and key issues that affected my progress.

Just to recap, the above is to emphasize one of the key cause elements to your liberation from drug addiction: Rebellion and keeping drug abuse a secret. The habit has to come out in the open so that it should not have power and dominance over you. And for you to have a willing heart to be corrected as an obedient child who truthfully seeks help for a better life and not to suffer or die prematurely. You must listen to the voice of God on the inside. I do not mean you have to go around telling or confessing to people about your condition or issues, it is not scriptural, religion has made this, not the word of God; it only says *"And the prayer [that is] of faith will save him who is sick, and the Lord will restore him; and if he has committed sins, he will be forgiven. Confess to one another therefore your faults (your slips, your false steps, your offenses, your sins) and pray [also] for one another, that you may be healed and restored [to a spiritual tone of mind and heart]. The earnest (heartfelt, continued) prayer of a righteous man makes tremendous power available [dynamic in its working]."*

Note that it *says "And the prayer of faith …"*; you only pray to God, so praying and confessing is to God. Then it says *"…Confess to one another your faults, your slips, your offenses (because we do these offenses and things physically to one another) … and pray for … that you may be healed"*; this is to those people in your life that you might have wronged or caused harm to. And subsequently, as a result of; a continued heartfelt prayer of a righteous man (a man in right standing with God, a man with righteousness consciousness) avails tremendous power (dynamic in its working); sorting out your issues in a dynamic way [closing doors to evil, healing every fiber of your being, repairing every aspect that concerns you, the list is endless].

In my case it was mainly my wife who was oblivious to drugs, she didn't know about it because I was concealing it, my actions were just too puzzling to her, and I was heavy on her and caused her much pain: physically and emotionally. I sincerely regret what I put her through, and repented. It is generally someone significant that has to know about it, and of cause, you have to let a pastor or church elder know about your dilemma so that they may pray with you.

Prayer of intercession is scriptural and has the power to help those we intercede for. Partners, parents, siblings, friends, and family need to take their rightful stand in corporate prayer for those who are addicted to substance abuse. This is reason enough to let those close to you know about your struggle with addiction so that they may gather together with you to take down this stronghold.

Jesus said, *"For where two or three are gathered in my Name, there Am I in the midst of them." Matthew 18:20*

Obedience leads to cleansing. When you are born again you are washed by the blood of Jesus, though not perfect in your walk (because your mind has to be renewed)and behavior, you just need to wash your feet with the word of God. We are being perfected.

John 13:10 Jesus said to him, "He who is bathed needs only to wash his feet, but is completely clean;"

He says remember then from what heights you have fallen. Repent (change the inner man to meet God's will) and do the works you did previously [when first you knew the Lord] - Revelation 2:5 AMP

"I see what you've done, your hard, hard work, your refusal to quit. I know you can't stomach evil, that you weed out apostolic pretenders. I know your persistence, your courage in my cause, that you never wear out. But you walked away from your first love-why? What's going on with you, anyway? Do you have any idea how far you've fallen? A Lucifer fall! Turn back! Recover your dear early love. No time to waste." - Revelation 2:2-5 MSG

Start living again, and doing well as you used to do. You have the power to choose to obey and learn; this is what you can do. The rest will follow.

Comprehend and Exercise Your Faith
- Faith means complete trust, unquestioning confidence; a strong belief
- Complete means having all its parts, entire, finished, total, thorough, in every way
- Trust is a firm belief in reliability or truth or strength etc. of a person or thing, state of being relied on; confident expectation; thing or person committed to one's care, resulting obligation, believe in, rely on character or behavior of, place reliance in, hope earnestly
- So we can explain faith as having an entire, total, thorough, finished firm belief in reliability, truth, and strength of a person, thing, or place with an earnest hope of results.

But how does God let us understand what faith is, that which is pleasing to Him? (that which is the core of our salvation)
  - *"Now **faith** is the **substance** of **things hoped** for, the **evidence** of **things not seen**." - Hebrews 11:1 KJV*

Let's look at this:

- o   substance is matter or material
- o   hope is expectation
- o   evidence is proof
- o   and things are belongings, clothes, equipment, possessions, effects, stuff, assets, liabilities, etc.
- o   Not seen is: not observable, not perceivable, and or not distinguishable to the naked eye or senses, but it is there, it exists

So faith is the material of belongings or possessions expected [so it's the material of that house I am expecting, that material that will cause the freedom I am expecting], the proof of belongings which are not perceivable to the naked eye [the title deed to the house which my eyes aren't designed to see, and the proof of my freedom from drugs which my eyes aren't designed to observe].

When you speak out loud by faith concerning something, you are creating or recreating whatever you want by using the building blocks, the material of that specific thing which you expect, and that in itself proof is created. The only difference is the dimension it's created in, the physical dimension can't comprehend the supernatural. Our senses, like the optical eyes, have a limited wavelength. As discussed in quantum mechanics, we can account for matter at the sub-atomic level though we can't see them. This is what I love about revelation knowledge, it opens your spiritual eye to understanding, and you then develop knowledge of reality and existence. Faith is our currency. It pleases God when you operate by faith in His likeness. I guess it would please me as well to see my child always having access to buying power.

"Now FAITH is the assurance (the confirmation, the title deed) of the things [we] hope for, being the proof of things [we] do not see and the conviction of their reality [faith perceiving as real fact what is not revealed to the senses]." - Hebrews 11:1 AMP

"By faith we understand that the worlds [during their successive ages] were framed (fashioned, put in order, and equipped for their intended purpose) by the word of God, so that what we see was not made out of things which are visible." - Hebrews 11:3 AMP

"God is not a man, that He should tell or act a lie," - Numbers 23:19 AMP

"And I say unto you, Ask, and it shall be given you; seek, and ye shall find; knock, and it shall be opened unto you. For every one that asketh receiveth; and he that seeketh findeth; and to him that knocketh it shall be opened. If a son shall ask bread of any of you that is a father, will he give him a stone? Or if he ask a fish, will he for a fish give him a serpent? Or if he shall ask an egg, will he offer him a scorpion? If ye then, being evil, know how to give good gifts unto your children: how much more shall your heavenly Father give the Holy Spirit to them that ask Him?" - Luke 11:9-13 KJV

Faith comes by hearing and hearing by the word of God, it is measurable, and you can increase it by meditating on God's word. The more you study the word, the more your faith will increase. And by faith, you will obtain good results.

We need to develop our faith so much as to have a total knowing. Take for instance the firm assurance we have towards sleeping and waking up; it is not common to see or hear of households having a commotion every night, people sweating with worry about what if they don't wake up tomorrow. Unless there are serious health issues. However we have this knowing beyond doubt, that we sleep without having to contemplate any disaster, we even plan around future dates. This is faith at its best but we hardly recognize it. We ought to be accustomed to experiencing success from faith in all avenues and be surprised when things don't work out, like a perfectly healthy person dying in their sleep. Then, when we question such mysteries we get taken to a higher knowing when we discover more truths. Like Paul said, "We *know* that *all things* work together for good to those who love the Lord."

"FOR WE know that if the tent which is our earthly home is destroyed (dissolved), we have from God a building, a house not made with hands, eternal in the heavens. Here indeed, in this [present abode, body], we sigh and groan inwardly, because we yearn to be clothed over [we yearn to put on our celestial body like a garment, to be fitted out] with our heavenly dwelling, So that by putting it on we may not be found naked (without a body). For while we are still in this tent, we groan under the burden and sigh deeply (weighed down, depressed, oppressed)—not that we want to put off the body (the clothing of the spirit), but rather that we would be further clothed, so that what is mortal (our dying body) may be swallowed up by life [after the resurrection]. Now He Who has fashioned us [preparing and making us fit] for this very thing is God, Who also has given us the [Holy] Spirit as a guarantee [of the fulfillment of His promise]. So then, we are always full of good and hopeful and confident courage; we know that while we are at home in the body, we are abroad from the home with the Lord [that is promised us]. For we walk by faith [we regulate our lives and conduct ourselves by our conviction or belief respecting man's relationship to God and holy fervor; thus we walk] not by sight or appearance. [Yes] we have confident and hopeful courage and are pleased rather to be away from home out of the body and be at home with the Lord.

Therefore, whether we are at home [on earth away from Him] or away from home [and with Him], we are constantly ambitious and strive earnestly to be pleasing Him. For we must all appear and be revealed as we are before the judgment seat of Christ, so that each one may receive [his pay] according to what he has done in the body, whether good or evil [considering what his purpose and motive have been, and what he has achieved, been busy with, and given himself and his attention to accomplishing].

Therefore, being conscious of fearing the Lord with respect and reverence, we seek to win people over [to persuade them]. But what sort of person we are is plainly recognized and thoroughly understood by God, and I hope that it is plainly recognized and understood also by your consciences (your inborn discernment). We are not commending ourselves to you again, but we are providing you with an occasion and incentive to be [rightfully] proud of us, so that you may have a reply for those who pride themselves on surface appearances [on the virtues they only appear to have], although their heart is devoid of them. For if we are beside ourselves [mad, as some say], it is for God and concerns Him; if we are in our right mind, it is for your benefit, For the love of Christ controls and urges and impels us, because we are of the opinion and conviction that [if] One died for all, then all died; And He died for all, so that all those who live might live no longer to and for themselves, but to and for Him Who died and was raised again for their sake. Consequently, from now on we estimate and regard no one from a [purely] human point of view [in terms of natural standards of value. [No] even though we once did estimate Christ from a human viewpoint and as a man, yet now [we have such knowledge of Him that] we know Him no longer [in terms of the flesh]." - 2 Corinthians 5:1-16 AMP

When you grasp this, the veil is taken off from the eyes of your understanding. You become aware of who you are, where you are positioned, and how you function. You are placed far above principalities and any corrupt nature. You are more than a conqueror through Christ. You are seated with Christ Jesus; you operate terrestrially as an ambassador to His kingdom. You are centered in and on love itself. You are hidden in Christ. And we don't believe in God because we have seen Him – it is by faith.

This is understanding *Life* prearranged and through being made the righteousness of God – you are awakened – God knew you before you were born. He has uniquely crafted you.

"For those whom He foreknew [of whom He was aware and loved beforehand], He also destined from the beginning [foreordaining them] to be molded into the image of His Son [and share inwardly His likeness], that He might become the firstborn among many brethren." - Romans 8:29 AMP

This has got nothing to do with stature, what you feel or perceive, educated or downtrodden, you are God's and He doesn't create flops. As long as you position yourself in His love your life will work out just fine.

We believe in God, and this is by a knowing in us and by faith. And when you receive Christ as your Lord and Savior, it's by faith. Your functionality at your core is all in faith and we comprehend what faith is. What faith says, so it is. When God looks at you he sees Jesus Christ in you; your hope of glory. So that's how you ought to look at yourself also. You have been reset: you are brand new. No one should tell you otherwise, if God says so, so it is.

Many people love God but suffer condemnation from their hearts through sin consciousness. You are concentrating and focusing on the wrong things you do (sin), and as a result, that focus enlarges sin then it becomes the ruling principle in your life and self-condemnation prevail. The more you ignore mistakes but take only lessons, the more they will dissipate and your actions and motives become driven by love.

Now that you are born again, do not be like a man that forgets who he is after looking in a mirror. Constantly be reminded who you are by the word of God. You become what you know from the word of God: from gnosis [general worldly and scientific knowledge] to epignosis; you become one with what you know: it's a process. For example, you will know that you are glorified by God, but your present situation doesn't agree with that. However, the more you study what the word says; the glorified of God, the more you hear it, the more your faith rises, the more the word increases in you, the more you speak words of power regenerating your body, recreating your world, then all the glorious attributes of what you speak starts gravitating into the physical realm, being visible to the naked eye. You start living in the inheritance God has promised to His seed. You are the seed according to the promise of God, the seed of Abraham. You are a joint heir with Christ Jesus. This will be evident to everyone, many will see the light you are.

Meditating on God's Word

"Meditate upon these things; give thyself wholly to them; that thy profiting may appear to all." - 1 Timothy 4:15 KJV

"This book of the law shall not depart out of thy mouth; but thou shall meditate on it day and night, that thou mayest observe to do according to all that is written therein: for then thou shalt make thy way prosperous, and then thou shalt have good success. Have not I commanded thee? Be strong and of a good courage; be not afraid, neither be thou dismayed: for the Lord thy God is with thee whithersoever thou goest." - Joshua 1:8-9 KJV

The resulting factor from meditation and acknowledgment of the above passages is seeing and having a clearer vision and improving in wisdom and knowledge of God. Yes, many will be astonished by what you have become.

"Now when they saw the boldness and unfettered eloquence of Peter and John and perceived that they were unlearned and untrained in the schools [common men with no educational advantages], they marveled; and they recognized that they had been with Jesus." - Acts 4:13 AMP

I cannot reiterate enough the power that is in the word of God; it is in itself the essence and nature of creation and re-creation of all things, which are, and to be, from the mouth of the possessor when projected out as sound (Speaking – out loud) - Rhema. The more you read, study, and look into the word of God, the more you are transformed into what it says.

"And all of us, as with unveiled face, [because we] continued to behold [in the Word of God] as in a mirror the glory of the Lord, are constantly being transfigured into His very own image in ever increasing splendor and from one degree of glory to another; [for this comes] from the Lord [Who is] the Spirit." 2 Corinthians 3:18 AMP

For instance, with repetition of the same scripture at different times and understanding thereof, you get multiple revelations about the very same message [example: 2 Corinthians 5:17 says if any man be in Christ, he is a new creature. What you initially understand from this is that your spirit is recreated and you are a new person. But later it will dawn on you that you are actually not a mere human being anymore, but a type of creature, altogether different to other types created: a being made in the class of God after the image of Christ Jesus], these are different dimension and reflects in one's growth – you move from one level of glory to the next and inevitably will reflect in your life. Please try, for your own sake, to read and study if you do not understand this mystery. The above scripture tells you Who the Creator of this Word is. [in the *Word of God … is the glory of the Lord, is His very own image*; for this *comes from the Lord (Who is) the Spirit.*]
"I said, You are gods [since you judge on My behalf, as My representatives]; indeed, all of you are children of the Most High." - Psalm 82:6 AMP

"May grace (God's favor) and peace (which is perfect well-being, all necessary good, all spiritual prosperity, and freedom from fears and agitating passions and moral conflicts) be multiplied to you in [the full, personal, precise, and correct] knowledge of God and of Jesus our Lord. For His divine power has bestowed upon us all things that [are requisite and suited] to life and godliness, through the [full, personal] knowledge of Him Who called us by and to His own glory and excellence (virtue).
By means of these He has bestowed on us His precious and exceedingly great promises, so that through them you may escape [by flight] from the moral decay (rottenness and corruption) that is in this world because of covetousness (lust and greed), and become sharers (partakers) of the divine nature. For this very reason, adding your diligence [to

the divine promise], employ every effort in exercising your faith to develop virtue (excellence, resolution, Christian energy), and in [exercising] virtue [develop] knowledge (intelligence),

And in [exercising] knowledge [develop] self-control, and in [exercising] self-control [develop] steadfastness (patience, endurance), and in [exercising] steadfastness [develop] godliness (piety), And in [exercising] godliness [develop] brotherly affection, and in [exercising] brotherly affection [develop] Christian love. For as these qualities are yours and increasingly abound in you, they will keep [you] from being idle or unfruitful unto the [full personal] knowledge of our Lord Jesus Christ (the Messiah, the Anointed One). For whoever lacks these qualities is blind, [spiritually] shortsighted, seeing only what is near to him, and has become oblivious [to the fact] that he was cleansed from his old sins. Because of this, brethren, be all the more solicitous and eager to make sure (to ratify, to strengthen, to make steadfast) your calling and election; for if you do this, you will never stumble or fall. Thus there will be richly and abundantly provided for you entry into the eternal kingdom of our Lord and Savior Jesus Christ." - 2 Peter 1:2-11 AMP

Advance from the general worldly and scientific knowledge to a more fuller, personal, precise, and correct knowledge of God and of Christ Jesus our Lord. You will become one with what you know, you will not only know and speak of it but be it: when they say you have that thing about you – the X Factor.

Confession:

I do not crave for drugs, I am free from addiction of any sort,
I have the life of God in me, I am more than a conqueror,
I live a victorious life, I am placed far above the devil and his principalities and the corrupt nature of this world,
I have arrived at a large place where I enjoy abundance of blessings,
God is my refuge and strength, my very present help,
God is the strength of my heart, and my portion forever,
The Lord is my salvation and my strength, I shall not fear,
That very same spirit that raised Jesus from the dead dwells in me, I have the resurrection spirit working in me,
My god maintainest my lot, he is the portion of my cup,
I am clothed with the garments of salvation, I am covered with the robe of righteousness,
I am glorified of God, I am justified of God, no weapon fashioned against me shall prosper for he that is in me is greater than he that is in the world,
Those who come against me fulfill their destiny, they have stumbled and they have fallen,
They will come in one direction but scatter in seven ways,
I function under grace, I have the favor of the living God
I am blessed and highly favored
God is able to make all grace abound towards me that I always have all sufficiency in all things may abound to every good work,
I am free from drug addiction in Jesus' Mighty Name Amen.

Be expectant of Results!!!

Rely On God's Love For You

Here I am the other day searching the word for understanding on prosperity: then God asked me how come you don't give Me a chance? The answer unraveled, showing me how unfair I've been to God. I remembered when I was expecting my son, I had prepared everything from diapers to toys that would last the guy till he was five years old. I had so much joy, not only that I was able to provide, but it was *my intention and will to do so*. But another question arose within me; how does it feel now when at times I don't have the budget to give my kids what they would like to have? It surely bothers me very much. Now God doesn't lack anything, but we constantly stand in the way of Him providing and blessing us; He loves us more than we can imagine – as a father or mother, do you think your child knows how much you love them?

"Now to Him Who, by (in consequence of) the [action of His] power that is at work within us, is able to [carry out His purpose and] do superabundantly, far over and above all that we [dare] ask or think [infinitely beyond our highest prayers, desires, thoughts, hopes, or dreams]" - Ephesians 3:20 AMP We all have a purpose as to why we are here on earth, and it is not a surprise why some are distracted by the enemy from accomplishing their divine destinies. It is the Father's will for His glory to be manifest in us.

We go about seeking satisfaction and worldly things propelled by our senses, and it shouldn't be, we miss the mark. Fulfillment is realized within our purposes, of which when we live therein, all things and all our heart's desires come as fringe benefits.

It is imperative to focus on one's life purpose, the things we are passionate about doing, which will profoundly impact other people and influence them positively. Evidence is all around us, athletes, musicians, producers, preachers, builders, lawyers, etc. We all have a part in the grand scheme of life, to be fulfilled through blessing others. The truth is these moments of satisfaction in helping others are achievable when we are anchored in our purposes. The lesser is included in the bigger.

We continue giving for this very reason. It is the joy and peace we get from charity work. The sooner you realize it the more you hold it dearly and live a purpose-driven life, but not from self-centeredness, but centered in Christ Jesus. When you rely on and trust in Jesus Christ, He is faithful to show you the way to all things that matters to your purpose. You will be content. You will be at peace beyond understanding, a kind that guards your heart and mind. As likened to the kind of military defense guarding a country, it will guard your domain.

Have a knowing inside you and boast of the love of God for you, He will show off about you to the whole world. Be confident that He that began a good work in you will finish it. It is not by your power nor is it by your will, but by His Spirit that lives in you. You are not alone, He said this Himself:

" ...*I will not in any way fail you nor give you up nor leave you without support. I will not, I will not, I will not in any degree leave you helpless nor forsake nor let you down (relax My hold on you)! [Assuredly not!]*" - *Hebrews 13:5 AMP*

Conclusion

Life is a precious gift, and gifts are presented for the fulfillment of joy. Do not walk about unconscious of this gift, you are a gift to the world, but you are not of this world. Now that you are in Christ, be the city on the mountaintop that cannot be hidden, let your light so shine!

God has put His Word above Himself (Psalm 138:2), it is your duty to use His Word. It has power and authority above all else, to cast down everything that claims to be greater.

What's impossible with man is possible with God, the limitation standards are lifted off: live from your spirit, a life lived by the principles ordained by the Wisdom of God. You are an ambassador of Zion, the city of the Most High God, deployed here terrestrially. Rules and principles of the dark world do not apply to you anymore. It is time to grow!

Remember to be persistent and relentless with the word of God. Think good and excellent thoughts, and use your imagination wisely – the future is now, stay focused on the image you see about yourself and yours. Speak those thoughts in line with God's word, be joyful in your creation, and do all you can and God will show up in your shortfall. Pray and fast when you require taking it by force. Learn of planting different seeds for different objectives in the kingdom and you will have multiple harvests.

Happy flourishing - In His presence is the fullness of joy, at His right-hand pleasures forevermore!!!

"For your shame ye shall have double; … all that see them shall acknowledge them, that they are the seed which the Lord hath blessed … For as the earth bringeth forth her bud, and as the garden causeth the things that are sown in it to spring forth; so the Lord God will cause righteousness and praise to spring forth before all the nations." - Isaiah 61:8-11 KJV

I say again, it is neither by might nor power, but by His Spirit.

"Now the Lord is the Spirit, and where the Spirit is, there is liberty (emancipation from bondage, freedom)." [Isa. 61:1, 2.] - 2 Corinthians 3:17 AMP

PS: It is not a coincidence you have this material in hand, God loves you, and do share His love.

Recognize and grow into Him: He *is* the Doer of God's work. He will finish what He has started in you.

May the grace of our Lord Jesus Christ and the sweet fellowship of the Holy Spirit rest and abide with us all the days of our lives as we dwell in the house of the Lord forever and ever. Stay blessed. Amen.